MEMORABLE WALKS IN
NEW YORK

5th Edition

Reid Bramblett

WILEY

Wiley Publishing, Inc.

Published by:

WILEY PUBLISHING, INC.
909 Third Ave.
New York, NY 10022

ISBN 0-7645-6744-6
ISSN 1081-339X

Editor: Elizabeth Albertson
Production Editor: Ian Skinnari
Photo Editor: Richard Fox
Cartographer: Elizabeth Puhl
Production by Wiley Indianapolis Composition Services

For information on our other products and services or to obtain technical support, please contact our Customer Care Department within the
U.S. at 800-762-2974, outside the U.S. at 317-572-3993 or fax
317-572-4002.

Wiley also publishes its books in a variety of electronic formats. Some
content that appears in print may not be available in electronic formats.

Manufactured in the United States of America

5   4   3   2   1

Contents

LIST OF MAPS

The Walking Tours

• • • • • • • • • • • • • • • • •

About the Author

Reid Bramblett is a veteran of the Frommer's editorial offices and the author of several Frommer's guides, including *Frommer's Italy from $70 a Day*, *Frommer's Tuscany and Umbria*, *Frommer's Northern Italy*, and *Europe For Dummies,* as well as a contributor to *Frommer's Europe from $70 A Day* and *Honeymoons For Dummies.* You'll notice the distinct lack of American destinations on that list of books. Never fear. Reid is also a former resident of Brooklyn's Park Slope and (briefly) Williamsburg neighborhoods, and he now hangs his hat in Maspeth, Queens. He promises one day to get around to living in Manhattan as well, but not until rents come way down or travel writers' salaries go way up.

Acknowledgments

I want to thank Liz Albertson for her fine editorial job, and for talking me into writing the new Harlem tour, which has now become one of my very favorite walks. Major props go out to my cousin Katy Hudnall, a newly-minted Manhattanite who eagerly accompanied me on many of the walks so as to get to know her new city (and ended up discovering the joys of schvitzing, an activity I don't believe they have in Atlanta). The brilliant and beautiful Frances Sayers, too, has helped walk several of the tours over the last few editions and braved the mysterious ingesting of unknown objects in the dim sum restaurants of Chinatown. I am, as always, humbly grateful to Margo Margolis, Marina Adams, and my father, Frank Bramblett—a trio of painters who have helped make sense of New York's gallery scene. And thanks, of course, to my mother, Karen Bramblett, who was the first to show me there was more to NYC than just the gallery scene!

An Invitation to the Reader

In researching this book, we discovered many wonderful places—hotels, restaurants, shops, and more. We're sure you'll find others. Please tell us about them, so we can share the information with your fellow travelers in upcoming editions. If you were disappointed with a recommendation, we'd love to know that, too. Please write to:

Frommer's Memorable Walks in New York, 5th Edition
Wiley Publishing, Inc.
909 Third Ave. • New York, NY 10022

An Additional Note

Please be advised that travel information is subject to change at any time—and this is especially true of prices. We therefore suggest that you write or call ahead for confirmation when making your travel plans. The authors, editors, and publisher cannot be held responsible for the experiences of readers while traveling. Your safety is important to us, however, so we encourage you to stay alert and be aware of your surroundings. Keep a close eye on cameras, purses, and wallets, all favorite targets of thieves and pickpockets.

FROMMERS.COM

Now that you have the guidebook to a great trip, visit our website at **www.frommers.com** for travel information on nearly 2,500 destinations. With features updated regularly, we give you instant access to the most current trip-planning information available. At Frommers.com, you'll also find the best prices on airfares, accommodations, and car rentals—and you can even book travel online through our travel booking partners. At Frommers.com, you'll also find the following:

- Online updates to our most popular guidebooks
- Vacation sweepstakes and contest giveaways
- Newsletter highlighting the hottest travel trends
- Online travel message boards with featured travel discussions

Introducing New York

Grasping the big picture of New York all at once is next to impossible. The best way to get to know this amazingly complex city is to do as New Yorkers do: Concentrate on small nooks and crannies rather than the whole. Define the city through its neighborhoods and pay close attention to every detail of architecture, image, and life.

As you explore, you'll run across tiny, funky flower gardens that have sprung up around sidewalk trees, a shop specializing in light bulbs, and a cafe concentrating on peanut butter. You'll find plaques identifying historic buildings and the former homes of famous people and ethnic food carts. Once you get away from the major museums and sights, you'll discover the Manhattan in which the rocks in Central Park acquire names, businessmen *schvitz* (Yiddish for sweat) in a Russian bathhouse, and Zabar's grocery store searches for a new unknown cheese from the Pyrenees to introduce to Upper West Siders.

That's why walking is truly the only way to see this city. To get anywhere near understanding New York, you need to grab just one chunk of it at a time, turn it over carefully in your mind, examine its history, and figure out what makes it tick. A large-scale New York may seem like an enormous, chaotic,

1

dirty, expensive, frightening metropolis. But on the small scale, in the details, New York gives up its secrets. It started as a conglomeration of small communities, and from these roots, it has grown into one of the most fascinating and vibrant cities on earth.

MIXED NUTS & MICHELANGELOS

A sizable cast of regular characters inhabits the city's streets. Strolling about, you might encounter the Tree Man, who is always festooned with leafy branches; the portly fellow with a long white beard who dresses as Santa Claus all year long (he's Jewish, no less); the Iguana Lady, whose hat is festooned with living reptiles; or the man who pushes a baby carriage with a large white duck inside.

Quentin Crisp once said, "Everyone in Manhattan is a star or a star manqué, and every flat surface in the island is a stage." Street performers run the gamut from a tuxedoed gent who does Fred-and-Ginger ballroom dances with a life-size rag doll (usually in front of the Metropolitan Museum) to the circus-caliber acrobats and stand-up comics who attract large audiences in Washington Square Park. Street musicians range from steel drum bands and Ecuadorean flute players to the pianist with his candelabra-adorned baby grand perched atop a truck.

Street artists abound. Here and there, especially in the East Village, little mosaic-tile designs pop up to adorn the sidewalk and streetlight pedestals. An area artist created them from cracked plates and crockery picked from people's trash.

In the 1980s, street painting became especially popular. Some sketched purple footsteps and stenciled animal and fish designs on sidewalks; others drew attention to the crime rate by painting body outlines all over the place. But in New York, nothing can remain small-time for long. Graffiti became an established art form, and the more highbrow street doodlers such as Keith Haring and Kenny Schraf became international stars.

TENEMENTS & TOWN HOUSES

New York is a city of extraordinarily diverse architecture. The Financial District's neoclassic "temples"—embellished with allegorical statuary, massive colonnades, vaulted domes, and

The Tours at a Glance

vast marble lobbies—stand side by side with the soaring skyscrapers that make up the world's most famous skyline.

The history of immigrant groups is manifest in the ramshackle tenements of Chinatown and the Lower East Side. SoHo's cast-iron facades hearken back to the ideals of the industrial era, when architectural design first encountered the principles of mass production and became accessible to everyone.

In Greenwich Village, you'll see the stately Greek Revival town houses where Henry James and Edith Wharton lived. Uptown, magnificent private mansions built for the Vanderbilts and the Whitneys, and gargantuan, tony apartment houses overlook Central Park, itself one of the world's most impressive urban greenbelts.

No wonder quintessential New Yorker Woody Allen was inspired to pay tribute to the city's architectural diversity by including an otherwise gratuitous tour of his favorite buildings in the movie *Hannah and Her Sisters.*

THE NEIGHBORHOODS: BOK CHOY, BEADS & BOHEMIANS

Though the city has been called more of a boiling pot than a melting pot, New Yorkers are proud of the ethnic diversity of the city's neighborhoods. From the days of the early Dutch settlers, immigrants have striven to re-create their native environments in selected neighborhoods. Hence, the restaurants of Mulberry Street, with convivial cafes spilling onto the sidewalks, evoke the streets of Palermo, and Orthodox Jews still operate shops that evolved from turn-of-the-20th-century pushcarts along cobblestoned Orchard Street.

Chinatown, home to more than 160,000 Chinese, is probably New York's most extensive ethnic area, and it's continually expanding, gobbling up parts of the old Lower East Side and Little Italy. Its narrow, winding streets are lined with noodle shops, Chinese vegetable vendors, small curio stores, Buddhist temples, Chinese movie theaters, and several hundred restaurants. New Yorkers don't talk about going out for Chinese food; they specify Sichuan, Hunan, Cantonese, Mandarin, Fukien, or dim sum.

The East Village has a sizable Ukrainian population, whose inexpensive restaurants (featuring borscht, blini, and pierogi) enhance the local culinary scene. Ukrainian folk arts, such as intricately painted Easter eggs, beautifully embroidered peasant blouses, and illuminated manuscripts, are displayed in local shops and even warrant a museum on Second Avenue.

There are Hispanic, Czech, German, Greek, Hungarian, Indian, Russian, Arab, and West Indian parts of town as well. But ethnic groups are not the only factor defining New York neighborhoods; commerce also delineates areas. On the streets around Broadway from Macy's to about 39th Street, you're in the heart of the Garment District, where artists race through the streets carrying large portfolios of next season's designs, trying not to collide with workers pushing racks of this year's fashions. Also distinct are the city's bead, book, feather, fur, flower, toy, diamond, and, of course, theater districts.

Different neighborhoods attract different residents. The Upper East Side is where old money lives; rumpled intellectuals prefer the Upper West Side. Young trendies and aging hippies live in the East Village; old bohemians live in the West Village. The West Village and Chelsea are home to sizable gay populations, and artists—and the yuppies who emulate them—hang out in SoHo and Chelsea. These are largely generalizations, of course, but each area does have a distinct flavor. You probably won't find designer clothing on St. Marks Place. On the other hand, a Madison Avenue boutique is unlikely to carry S&M leather wear. Midtown is the city's main shopping area, the site of ever-diminishing grand department stores. Broadway dissects the town diagonally; though it's most famous for the glitz and glitter of the Great White Way, it spans Manhattan from Battery Park to the Bronx.

IF YOU CAN MAKE IT HERE . . .

The song has become a cliché, but like many clichés it's true. New York is, and always has been, a mecca for the ambitious. And though only a small percentage of the ardently aspiring become famous—or even manage to eke out a living—the effort keeps New Yorkers keen-witted, intense, and on the cutting edge.

New York is America's business and financial center, where major deals have gone down over power lunches since the days when Thomas Jefferson and Alexander Hamilton chose the site for the nation's capital over a meal at a Manhattan restaurant. Every major book and magazine publisher is based here. It's an international media and fashion center as well. New York galleries set worldwide art trends. And a lead in a play in Galveston, Texas, is less impressive than a bit part on Broadway. (At least New Yorkers think so.)

For that reason, it seems that almost every famous artist, writer, musician, and actor has, at one time or another, resided in Gotham. The waitress serving you in a coffee shop may be tomorrow's Glenn Close; your cab driver may make the cover of *Time*. And because they're all over town, you'll probably even rub elbows with an already-acclaimed celebrity or two as well. If not, there's always the thrill of downing a drink or two in bars that Dylan Thomas or Jackson Pollock frequented, visiting the Greenwich Village haunts of the Beat Generation, peering up at what was once Edgar Allan Poe's bedroom window, or dining at the Algonquin Hotel where Round Table wits Dorothy Parker, Alexander Woollcott, and George S. Kaufman traded barbs in the 1920s.

The presence of so many movers and shakers gives New York vitality and sophistication. When you study film at the New School, your lecturers are Martin Scorsese, Sydney Pollack, Barry Levinson, and Neil Simon. Pavarotti is at one Met (the Metropolitan Opera), and everyone from Raphael to Rembrandt is at the other. Few bookstores are as great as the Strand, no food shop is as alluring as Zabar's (except perhaps Balducci's or Dean and Deluca), no department store is a match for Bloomie's and Macy's, and no mall is comparable to Orchard Street. Where else can you easily satisfy a craving for Thai noodles at 3am? Or have your choice of dozens of art-house and foreign movies on the big screen nightly, many of which will never play in most American towns?

Visitors often question how New Yorkers stand the constant noise, the rudeness, the filth, the outrageous rents and prices, the crime, the crazies, or even one another. But though New Yorkers frequently talk about leaving the city, few ever do. They've created a unique frame of reference, and it doesn't travel well. The constant stimulation feeds Gothamites' creativity. To quote theatrical impresario Joseph Papp, "Creative people get inspiration from their immediate environment, and New York has the most immediate environment in the world."

Lower Manhattan/ The Financial District

Start: Battery Park/U.S. Customs House.

Subway: Take the 4 or 5 to Bowling Green, the 1 or 9 to South Ferry, or the N or R to Whitehall Street.

Finish: The Municipal Building.

Time: Approximately 3 hours.

Best Time: Any weekday, when the wheels of finance are spinning and lower Manhattan is a maelstrom of activity.

Worst Time: Weekends, when most buildings and all the financial markets are closed.

The narrow winding streets of the Financial District occupy the earliest-settled area of

Manhattan, where Dutch settlers established the colony of Nieuw Amsterdam in the early 17th century. Before their arrival, downtown was part of a vast forest, a lush hunting ground for Native Americans that was inhabited by mountain lions, bobcats, beavers, white-tailed deer, and wild turkeys. A hunting path, which later evolved into Broadway, extended from the Battery to the present City Hall Park.

Today this section of the city centers on commerce, much as Nieuw Amsterdam did. Wall Street is America's strongest symbol of money and power; bulls and bears have replaced the wild beasts of the forest, and conservatively-attired lawyers, stockbrokers, bankers, and businesspeople have supplanted the Native Americans and Dutch who once traded otter skins and beaver pelts on these very streets.

A highlight of this tour is the Financial District's architecture, in which the neighborhood's modern edifices and grand historical structures are dramatically juxtaposed: Colonial, 18th-century Georgian/Federal, and 19th-century neoclassical buildings stand in the shadow of colossal modern skyscrapers.

Much changed on September 11, 2001, when Lower Manhattan lost its greatest landmark; New York lost a familiar chunk of its skyline, America lost a share of its innocence, and more than 2,700 people lost their lives as a pair of planes commandeered by Osama bin Laden's Al Qaeda terrorists plowed into the Twin Towers of the World Trade Center. Those horrific events have etched themselves into all our memories. Nothing I can say here can do justice to the heroism of the firefighters and other emergency workers who rushed into the burning buildings to help, only to perish when the towers collapsed. All I can do is invite all of you to come to New York, visit Lower Manhattan, pay your respects at ground zero, and see how energetically, stubbornly, and wonderfully New York and its citizens are bouncing back from the tragedy.

• • • • • • • • • • • • • • • •

The subways mentioned above all exit in or near **Battery Park,** an expanse of green at Manhattan's tip which rests entirely upon a landfill—an old strategy of the Dutch to expand their settlement farther into the bay. The original tip of Manhattan ran along Battery Place, which borders

Lower Manhattan/The Financial District

1 U.S. Customs House
2 Bowling Green Park
3 Cunard Building
4 Fraunces Tavern Museum
5 New York Stock Exchange
6 Federal Hall National Memorial
7 Wall Street
8 Trinity Church
9 Jean Dubuffet's *Group of Four Trees*
10 Isamu Noguchi's 1967 *The Red Cube*
11 Ground Zero
12 Kalikow Building
13 St. Paul's Chapel
14 Woolworth Building
15 City Hall Park
16 City Hall
17 Tweed Courthouse
18 Surrogate's Court
(The Hall of Records)
19 The Municipal Building

the north side of the park. State Street flanks the park's east side, and stretched along it, filling the space below Bowling Green, is the beaux arts bulk of the old:

1. **U.S. Customs House,** home to the Smithsonian's National Museum of the American Indian (☎ 212/668-6624; www.si.edu/nmai) since 1994. The giant statues lining the front of this granite 1907 structure personify Asia (pondering philosophically), America (bright-eyed and bushy-tailed), Europe (decadent, whose time has passed), and Africa (sleeping) and were carved by Daniel Chester French of Lincoln Memorial fame. The most interesting, if unintentional, sculptural statement—keeping in mind the building's new purpose—is the giant seated woman to the left of the entrance, representing America. The young, upstart America is surrounded by references to Native America: Mayan pictographs on her throne, Quetzalcoatl (an Aztec god symbolized by a feathered serpent) under her foot, a shock of corn in her lap, and a Plains Indian scout over her shoulder. Look behind her throne for the stylized crow figure. The crow is an important animal in many native cultures, usually playing a trickster character in myths, which is probably why it's hiding in this sculpture.

The airy oval rotunda inside was frescoed by Reginald Marsh to glorify the shipping industry (and, by extension, the customs office once here). I highly recommend the free museum, open daily 10am to 5pm (to 8pm Thurs), which hosts a roster of well-curated exhibits highlighting Native American cultures, history, and contemporary issues in sophisticated and thought-provoking ways.

As you exit the building, directly in front of you sits the pretty little oasis of:

Kid-Friendly Experiences

- Visiting the National Museum of the American Indian in the old U.S. Customs House (stop 1)
- Riding the Bronze Bull on Broadway (after stop 3)
- Experiencing history at Federal Hall (stop 6)

2. **Bowling Green Park.** In 1626, Dutchman Peter Minuit stood at this spot (or somewhere close to it) and gave glass beads and other trinkets worth about 60 guilders ($24) to a group of Indians, and claimed that he had thereby bought Manhattan. However, the local Indians didn't consider that they owned this island in the first place because Manhattan (*Mantay* in local Delaware language means "the island") was a communal hunting ground that was shared by several different groups. (The idea that the Indians didn't believe in property is a colonial myth; the Indians had their own territories nearby.) It isn't clear what the Indians thought the trinkets meant. Either (a) they just thought the exchange was a formal way, one to which they were accustomed, of closing an agreement to extend the shared hunting use of the island to this funny-looking group of pale people with yellow beards, or (b) they were knowingly selling land that they didn't own in the first place and thus performing the first shrewd real-estate deal of the Financial District. They probably then told Minuit that they also had this bridge to sell, just up the river a ways, but he was too busy fortifying his little town of Nieuw Amsterdam to listen. There's evidence that the "sellers" of Manhattan were of the Canarsie tribe from what is today Brooklyn.

Although Bowling Green Park today is just another lunch spot for stockbrokers, when King George III repealed the hated Stamp Act in 1770, New Yorkers magnanimously raised a statue of him here. The statue lasted 5 years, until the day the *Declaration of Independence* was read to the public in front of City Hall (now Federal Hall) up the street and a crowd rushed down Broadway to topple the statue, chop it up, melt it down, and transform it into 42,000 bullets with which to shoot the British.

The park also marks the start of Broadway—which, if you follow it far enough, leads to Albany. Walk up the left side of Broadway; at no. 25 is the:

3. **Cunard Building.** In 1921, this present-day post office was the ticketing room for Cunard, one of the world's most glamorous shipping and cruise lines and the proprietor of the *QEII*. Cunard established the first passenger steamship between Europe and the Americas, and in this

still-impressive Great Hall, you once could book passage on one of their famous ships, such as the *QEI* or the *Lusitania.* The poorly lit and deteriorating churchlike ceiling inside (the building is open Mon–Fri 6am–7pm, Sat 6am–1:30pm) is covered with Ezra Winter paintings of the ships of Columbus, Sir Francis Drake, and Leif Eriksson, among others.

As you exit the building, cross to the traffic island to pat the enormous **bronze bull,** symbol of a strong stock market that is ready to charge up Broadway. This instant icon began as a practical joke by Italian sculptor Arturo DiModica, who originally stuck it in front of the New York Stock Exchange building in the middle of the night in 1989. The unamused brokers had it promptly removed, and it was eventually placed here.

Turn right to head south on Broadway, on the left side of the U.S. Customs House on Whitehall Street. Take a left onto Pearl Street; just past Broad Street stretches a historic block lined with (partially rebuilt) 18th- and 19th-century buildings. The two upper stories of 54 Pearl St. house the:

4. **Fraunces Tavern Museum** (☎ 212/425-1778), where you can view the room in which Washington's historic farewell to his officers took place on December 4, 1783 (today, it's set up to represent a typical 18th-century tavern room) and see other American history exhibits. A small admission fee is charged. Hours are Tuesday, Wednesday, and Friday from 10am to 5pm, Thursday from 10am to 7pm, and Saturday from 11am to 5pm. The restaurant installed in the posh, oak-paneled dining room and adjacent pub emerged from several years of extensive renovations in the fall of 2001, which inexplicably did away with much of the wonderful old clubby feel of the place, leaving it with a rather staid and uninspired decor. The food's good, but pricey.

From Fraunces Tavern, head straight up Broad Street past all the chain lunch spots that cater to harried brokers. At no. 20, on the left, is the main entrance to the:

5. **New York Stock Exchange** (☎ 212/656-5168; www. nyse.com), which is near the buttonwood tree where

merchants met as long ago as 1792 to try and pass off to each other the U.S. bonds that had been sold to fund the Revolutionary War. By 1903, they were trading stocks of publicly held companies in this Corinthian-columned, beaux arts "temple" designed by George Post. Close to 2,500 companies are listed on the exchange, where they trade 79 billion shares valued around $4.5 trillion.

Sadly, the new security measures have put at least a temporary stop to letting visitors inside the exchange for a tour and to peer out over the bustling trading floor from an observation deck where Abbie Hoffman and Jerry Rubin once created chaos by tossing dollar bills onto the exchange floor in the 1960s. Check the website above to see if visits have been green-lighted.

Continue north (left) up Broad Street. At the end of the block, you'll see the Parthenon-inspired:

6. **Federal Hall National Memorial,** 26 Wall St. at Nassau Street (☎ **212/825-6888;** www.nps.gov/feha). Fronted by 32-foot fluted marble Doric columns, this imposing 1842 neoclassical temple is built on the site of the British City Hall building, later called Federal Hall. Peter Zenger, publisher of the outspoken *Weekly Journal,* stood trial in 1735 for "seditious libel" against Royal Gov. William Cosby. Defended brilliantly by Alexander Hamilton, Zenger was eventually acquitted (based on the grounds that anything that is printed that is true, even if it isn't very nice, can't be construed as libel), and his acquittal set the precedent for freedom of the press, later guaranteed in the Bill of Rights, which was drafted and signed inside this building.

New York's first major rebellion against British authority occurred here when the Stamp Act Congress met in 1765 to protest King George III's policy of "taxation without representation." J. Q. A. Ward's 1883 statue of George Washington on the steps commemorates the spot of the first presidential inauguration in 1789. Congress met here after the revolution, when New York was briefly the nation's capital.

Exhibits within (open Mon–Fri 9am–5pm) illuminate these events along with other aspects of American history. Admission is free.

Facing Federal Hall, turn left up the road that has become the symbol of high finance the world over:

7. **Wall Street.** This narrow street, which is just a few short blocks long, started out as a service road that ran along the fortified wall that the Dutch erected in 1653 to defend against Indian attack. (Gov. Peter Stuyvesant's settlers had at first played off tribes against each other in order to trick them into ceding more and more land, but the native groups quickly realized that their real enemies were the Dutch.)

Wall Street hits Broadway across the street from:

8. **Trinity Church** (☎ 212/602-0800; www.trinitywall street.org). Serving God and mammon, this Wall Street house of worship—with neo-Gothic flying buttresses, beautiful stained-glass windows, and vaulted ceilings—was designed by Richard Upjohn and consecrated in 1846. At that time, its 280-foot spire dominated the skyline. Its main doors, embellished with biblical scenes, were inspired in part by Ghiberti's famed doors on Florence's Baptistery. An earlier church on this site was built in 1697 and burned down in 1776.

The church runs a brief tour daily at 2pm. A small museum at the end of the left aisle displays documents (including the 1697 church charter from King William III), photographs, replicas of the Hamilton-Burr duel pistols, and other items. Capt. James Lawrence, whose famous last words were, "Don't give up the ship," and Alexander Hamilton are buried in the churchyard (against the south fence, next to steamboat inventor Robert Fulton), where the oldest grave dates from 1681.

Thursdays at 1pm, Trinity holds its Noonday Concert series of chamber music and orchestral concerts. Call ☎ 212/602-0747 for details.

Take a left out of the church and walk two short blocks up Broadway. As you pass Cedar Street, look (don't walk) to your right, across Broadway, and down Cedar Street. At the end of the street, you'll see:

9. **Jean Dubuffet's Group of Four Trees.** Installed in 1972, these amorphous mushroomlike white shapes traced with undulating black lines are representative of

the artist's patented style. Dubuffet considered these installations as drawings in three dimensions "which extend and expand into space."

Closer at hand, in front of the tall, black Marine Midlank Bank building on Broadway between Cedar and Liberty streets, is:

10. **Isamu Noguchi's 1967 The Red Cube,** another famed outdoor sculpture of downtown Manhattan. Noguchi fancied that this rhomboid "cube" balancing on its corner and shot through with a cylinder of empty space represented chance, like the "rolling of the dice." This sculpture is appropriately located in the gilt-edged gambling den that is the Financial District.

As you're looking at *The Red Cube* across Broadway, turn around to walk down Liberty Plaza/Liberty Street toward the big gaping hole in the fabric of Manhattan:

11. **Ground Zero,** the eerie, somber hole in the ground where the World Trade Center once stood. For a sense of what was lost, here are some of the statistics that described the World Financial Center: Opened in 1970 under the auspices of the Port Authority, this immense complex covered 12 million square feet of rentable office space housing more than 350 firms and organizations. About 50,000 people worked in its precincts, and some 70,000 others (tourists and businesspeople) visited each day. The complex included the 110-story Twin Towers, a sleek 22-story Marriott Hotel, a plaza the size of four football fields, artworks by Calder and Miró (Calder's sculpture was pulled out of the rubble remarkably intact), an underground shopping mall, and several restaurants, most notably the spectacular Windows on the World, where you could dine 1,377 feet above the ground. We'll miss it all.

Take a Break You can get a unique perspective on the World Trade Center site by heading around to the west side of the site to the **World Financial Center's Winter Garden.** This enormous, 120-foot-high glass-and-steel atrium featuring 45-foot palms from the Mojave Desert offers varied dining choices—everything from pub fare to gourmet pizzas. The east side has a glass wall and an indoor terrace of sorts that overlooks the World Trade

Center site. The lower, west side overlooks a yacht harbor and a pleasant cement park and has outdoor tables available, weather permitting.

Continue north on Church Street to turn right down Dey Street back to Broadway. Take a left, and on your left is the:

12. **Kalikow Building,** 195 Broadway. This neoclassic tower that dates from 1915 to 1922 is the former headquarters of AT&T and has more exterior columns than any other building in the world. The 25-story structure rests on a Doric colonnade, with Ionic colonnades above. The lobby evokes a Greek temple with a forest of massive fluted columns. The building's tower crown is modeled on the Mausoleum of Halicarnassus, a great Greek monument of antiquity. The bronze panels over the entranceway by Paul Manship (sculptor of Rockefeller Center's Prometheus) symbolize wind, air, fire, and earth.

Continue north on Broadway. The next block, between Vesey and Fulton streets, contains the small:

13. **St. Paul's Chapel** (☎ 212/602-0872; www.saintpauls chapel.org). Dating from 1764, this is New York's only surviving pre-Revolutionary church. Under the east portico is a 1789 monument to Gen. Richard Montgomery, one of the first Revolutionary patriots to die in battle. During the 2 years that New York was the nation's capital, George Washington worshiped at this Georgian chapel belonging to Trinity Church; his pew is on the right side of the church. Built by Thomas McBean, with a temple-like portico and fluted Ionic columns supporting a massive pediment, the chapel resembles London's St. Martin's-in-the-Fields. Explore the small graveyard where 18th- and early-19th-century notables rest in peace and modern businesspeople sit for lunch. In the months following the September 11, 2001, terrorist attacks, the chapel became a center for the workers and volunteers to wash up, get something to eat or drink, nap on the pews or on cots, and receive relief in the form of free chiropractic care, massages, and, of course, spiritual counseling. Trinity's Noonday Concert series is held here each Monday, at noon, featuring a variety of musical performances, from Japanese koto players to brass quartets.

Continue up Broadway, crossing Vesey and Barclay streets, and at 233 Broadway is the:

14. **Woolworth Building.** This soaring "cathedral of commerce" cost Frank W. Woolworth $13.5 million worth of nickels and dimes in 1913. Designed by Cass Gilbert, it was the world's tallest edifice until 1930, when the Chrysler Building surpassed it. At its opening, President Woodrow Wilson pressed a button from the White House that illuminated the building's 80,000 electric bulbs. The neo-Gothic architecture is rife with spires, gargoyles, flying buttresses, vaulted ceilings, 16th-century–style stone-as-lace traceries, castlelike turrets, and a churchlike interior.

    Step into the lofty marble entrance arcade to view the gleaming mosaic, Byzantine-style ceiling, and gold-leafed, neo-Gothic cornices. The corbels (carved figures under the crossbeams) in the lobby include whimsical portraits of the building's engineer Gunwald Aus measuring a girder (above the staircase to the left of the main door), designer Gilbert holding a miniature model of the building, and Woolworth counting coins (both above the left-hand corridor of elevators). Stand near the security guard's central podium and crane your neck for a glimpse at Paul Jennewein's murals of Commerce and Labor, half hidden up on the mezzanine.

    To get an overview of the Woolworth Building's architecture, cross Broadway. On this side of the street, you'll find scurrying city officials and growing greenery that together make up:

15. **City Hall Park,** a 250-year-old green surrounded by landmark buildings. A Frederick MacMonnies statue near the southwest corner of the park depicts Nathan Hale at age 21, having just uttered his famous words before execution: "I only regret that I have but one life to lose for my country." Northeast of City Hall in the park is a statue of *New York Tribune* founding editor Horace Greeley (seated with newspaper in hand) by J. Q. A. Ward. This small park has been a burial ground for paupers and the site of public executions, parades, and protests.

    It now provides the setting for:

16. **City Hall,** the seat of the municipal government, housing the offices of the mayor and his staff, the city council, and other city agencies. City Hall combines Georgian and French Renaissance styles and was designed by Joseph F. Mangin and John McComb Jr. from 1803 to 1811. Later additions include the clock and 6,000-pound bell in the cupola tower. The cupola itself is crowned with a stately, white-painted copper statue of Justice (anonymously produced in a workshop).

    Barring days when there are demonstrations or special hearings that draw large crowds, you can enter the building between 10am and 4pm, Monday to Friday. Several areas are open to the public, including the Corinthian-columned lobby, which centers on a coffered and skylit rotunda. You can set up tours if there are more than 13 people in your group. The elegant Governor's Room upstairs, where Lafayette was received in 1824, houses a museum containing Washington's writing desk, his inaugural flag, and artwork by well-known American artists. This room is closed from noon to 1pm. City Hall contains quite an impressive collection of American art; in your wanderings, you might note works by George Caitlin, Thomas Sully, Samuel B. Morse, and Rembrandt Peale, among others.

    Along the north edge of City Hall Park on Chambers Street sits the now shabby:

17. **Tweed Courthouse** (New York County Courthouse, 52 Chambers St.). This 1872 Italianate courthouse was built during the tenure of William Marcy "Boss" Tweed, who, in his post on the board of supervisors, stole millions in construction funds. Originally budgeted as a $250,000 job in 1861, the courthouse project escalated to the staggering sum of $14 million. Bills were padded to an unprecedented extent—Andrew Garvey, who was to become known as the "Prince of Plasterers," was paid $45,966.89 for a single day's work! The ensuing scandal (Tweed and his cronies were discovered to have pocketed at least $10 million) wrecked Tweed's career; he died penniless in jail.

Across Chambers Street and to the right, at the corner of Elk Street, lies the turn-of-the-20th-century:

18. **Surrogate's Court (The Hall of Records),** 31 Chambers St. Housed in this sumptuous beaux arts structure are all the legal records relating to Manhattan real estate deeds and court cases, some dating from the mid-1600s. Heroic statues of distinguished New Yorkers (Peter Stuyvesant, De Witt Clinton, and others) front the mansard roof. The doorways, surmounted by arched pediments, are flanked by Philip Martiny's sculptural groups portraying New York in Revolutionary Times (to your left) and New York in Its Infancy (to your right). Above the entrance is a three-story Corinthian colonnade.

Step inside to see the vestibule's beautiful barrel-vaulted mosaic ceiling, embellished with astrological symbols, Egyptian and Greek motifs, and figures representing retribution, justice, sorrow, and labor. Continue back to the two-story sky-lit neoclassical atrium, clad in honey-colored marble with a colonnaded second-floor loggia and an ornate staircase adapted from the foyer of the Grand Opera House in Paris.

Exiting the Surrogate's Court from the front door, you'll see to your left, at the end of the block, that Chambers Street disappears under:

19. **The Municipal Building,** a grand civic edifice built between 1909 and 1914 to augment City Hall's government office space. The famed architectural firm of McKim, Mead, and White (as in Stanford White) used Greek and Roman design elements such as a massive Corinthian colonnade, ornately embellished vaults and cornices, and allegorical statuary in their design for this building. A triumphal arch, its barrel-vaulted ceiling adorned with relief panels, forms a magnificent arcade over Chambers Street; this arch has been called the "gate of the city." Sculptor Adolph Weinman created many of the building's bas-reliefs, medallions, and allegorical groupings of human figures (they symbolize civic pride, progress, guidance, prudence, and executive power). Weinman also designed the heroic hammered-copper

statue of Civic Fame that tops the Municipal Building 582 feet above the street. This statue, which is the largest one in Manhattan, holds a crown with five turrets that represent New York's five boroughs.

See lots of lovey-dovey couples walking in and out? The city's marriage license bureau is on the second floor, and a wedding takes place about every 20 minutes.

Chinatown

Start: The intersection of Broadway and Canal Street.

Subway: Take the 6, N, R, J, M, or Z to Canal Street.

Finish: The intersection of East Broadway and Rutgers Street.

Time: 2 to 3 hours, not including restaurant stops.

Best Time: Anytime the weather is good for walking.

The main draw in Chinatown is the food; the neighborhood's 400-odd restaurants have satisfied New Yorkers' cravings for Cantonese, Hunan, and Szechuan fare, as well as Thai and Vietnamese cuisines, for many years. Outside the doors of the restaurants, the swirling, exotic street life of one of the largest Chinese communities in the Western Hemisphere awaits. In the shops along Mott, Canal, and East Broadway, you'll find unusual foodstuffs, Chinese herbal medicines, and collectibles that you'd think only a trip to Hong Kong or Shanghai could net. In Chinatown's narrow streets and aging tenements, you can discover the legacies of the different waves of immigrants—first the English, then the Germans, Irish, Italians, Jews, and finally, the Chinese.

Although East Indies trading ships brought small groups of Chinese to New York from about 1840 on, Chinatown did not really begin to develop until the 1880s. Thousands of

Chinese sailed to California in the mid–19th century, hoping to amass fortunes by working the mines and building railroads, and return to China rich men. By the 1870s, they became the victims of a tide of racism, violence, and legal persecution throughout the West. In 1882, Congress passed the Chinese Exclusion Act, which denied the Chinese the right to citizenship, barred them from most occupations, and suspended immigration. Additionally, the act forbade any laborers already in the country from bringing their wives here. Some Chinese returned home, but tens of thousands remained. From 1880 to 1890, the Chinese population on Mott, Pell, and Doyers streets increased tenfold to 12,000.

By the 1890s, Chinatown had become a large and isolated ghetto, and it remained so for many years. Since World War II, however, the neighborhood has been building bridges to the American mainstream. A large influx of foreign capital from Taiwan and Hong Kong has helped make Chinatown one of New York's strongest local economies, and many Chinese Americans have joined the middle class. But unlike other famous immigrant neighborhoods such as Little Italy or the Lower East Side, Chinatown isn't ready to be relegated to the history books—immigrants from all parts of Asia continue to stream in, adding new energy and color to the neighborhood.

• • • • • • • • • • • • • • • •

Start off walking east along Canal Street. You'll probably have to thread your way through a multiethnic throng of pedestrians and street vendors hawking toys, firecrackers, and dumplings—Canal Street during business hours is one of New York's most frenzied, crowded thoroughfares. From Broadway to the Bowery, Canal Street is lined with bustling variety stores, fish markets, greengrocers, banks, and Chinese-owned jewelry shops. Many of the storefronts have been subdivided into minimalls whose stalls purvey everything from ginseng to martial arts paraphernalia. However, when night falls and the shops are shuttered, Canal Street seems like a ghost town in the hills of China.

You'll see plenty of Chinese-language signs on Canal Street as soon as you walk east of Broadway. The landmark that signals your arrival in Chinatown proper is the former:

Chinatown

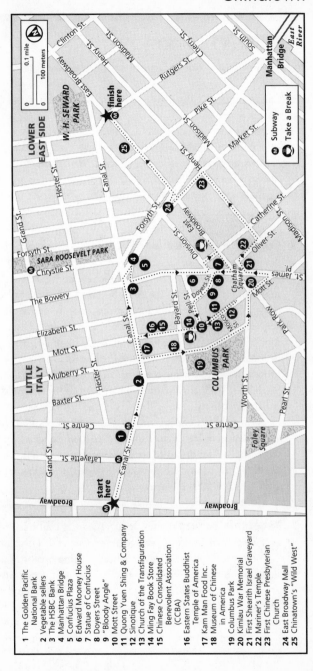

Kid-Friendly Experiences

- Learning the violent history of the "Bloody Angle" (stop 9)
- Shopping for Chinatown souvenirs at the shops on Mott Street (stop 10)
- Sampling the goodies at Aji Ichiban candy store (see the "Take a Break" box on p. 31)
- Browsing Chinese groceries at Kam Man Food, Inc. (stop 17)
- Exploring Columbus Park (stop 19)

1. **Golden Pacific National Bank.** Located on the northwest corner of Canal and Centre streets, this building was raised in 1983 as the bank's new home. At first a major point of pride in the neighborhood, the bank failed only 2 years later, and its patrons, largely individual Chinese, lost their uninsured deposits. The colorful building, with a jade-trimmed red pagoda roof and elaborately decorated facade with Oriental phoenix and dragon motifs, has been resurrected as . . . wait for it . . . a Starbucks. Walk around on Centre Street to see the building in its entirety.

   Although this one is defunct, Canal Street is still lined with banks; indeed Chinatown's 161,000 residents are served by several dozen of them, more than most cities of similar size. Many Chinatown residents routinely put away 30% to 50% of their wages.

   Continue east along Canal Street and look for:

2. **Vegetable sellers** plying their trade on a traffic island at Baxter Street. Here you can peruse and purchase Chinese produce: bok choy (delicate Chinese cabbage), small white and red-violet eggplants, taro root, fresh ginger, Chinese squash, big white winter melons, tender bamboo shoots, yard-long green beans, pale golden lily buds, lotus leaves, cucumber-sized okras, and sweet snow peas. (There are more stalls just up around the corner on Mulberry St.)

Cross from the traffic island to the southern side of Canal Street where you'll smell a briny aroma emanating from a fish market (nos. 218 and 214) whose ice-covered offerings spill out onto the sidewalk. The aproned fish sellers keep up a steady patter, extolling the virtues of their shark, squid, snapper, oysters, and live eels, frogs, and snakes. Here and throughout your tour of Chinatown, you'll also pass carts vending Peking duck, chicken feet, roast pork, and lo mein, as well as store windows displaying barbecued chickens, ducks, and squab with heads and beaks fully intact.

Soak up the street scene as you continue up Canal for several more bustling, crowded blocks to the southwest corner of Canal Street and the Bowery. Here, at 58 Bowery, you'll find a branch of:

3. **The HSBC Bank.** Built in 1924, and later overhauled and tailored to its Chinese depositors, this dome-roofed bank is one of New York's most distinctive. (It's hard to appreciate from directly underneath; cross Canal for a better view.) Its interior is decorated with tondos (round paintings) extolling Wisdom, Thrift, Success, and Safety.

Across the Bowery to the east is the approach to the:

4. **Manhattan Bridge.** This suspension bridge, built in 1905, may not be as inspirational to poets and artists as the great Brooklyn Bridge, but the monumental beaux arts colonnade and arch that stand at its entrance are quite grand and arresting.

Looming to the right of the bridge, on the east side of the Bowery, is:

5. **Confucius Plaza.** The first major publicly funded housing project built for Chinese use, Confucius Plaza extends from Division Street up to the Bowery, where it rises into a curved 43-story tower.

The activist spirit of the 1960s touched Chinatown in a significant way: Many young people from the neighborhood were involved in a Chinese-American pride movement and created organizations devoted to building community centers, providing social services, and securing Chinatown a voice in city government. Winning the fight to build this plaza and forcing contractors to hire Chinese workers showed that Chinatown was now a political heavy hitter.

Walk south on the Bowery to building no. 18, which sits on the southeast corner of the Bowery and Pell Street and is called the:

6. **Edward Mooney House** (occupied by Summit Mortgage Bankers). This largely Georgian brick row house, painted red with eggshell trim, dates from George Washington's New York days. It was built in 1785 on property abandoned by a Tory during the Revolution and is the oldest Georgian brick row house in the city.

The Bowery ends at Chatham Square, into which nine other streets converge. On a traffic island to your left, you'll see the:

7. **Statue of Confucius.** Raised in 1976, this bronze statue and its green marble base were gifts of the Chinese Consolidated Benevolent Association (CCBA), which has served as Chinatown's unofficial government for more than 100 years. The organization has always represented conservative Chinese who support traditional notions of family loyalty and respect for one's elders and leaders; the statue was built over the strenuous objections of activist groups who felt that the neighborhood should display a more progressive cultural symbol. However, the sage's 2,400-year-old words, inscribed in the monument's base in both Chinese and English, are strikingly descriptive of the strength of Chinatown's tightknit social fabric: Confucius recommends that we look beyond our immediate family and see all elders as our parents and all children as our own.

From the statue of Confucius, follow Catherine Street past the pagoda-roofed Republic Bank for Savings and turn left onto East Broadway. This thoroughfare is the heart of commercial, workday Chinatown. Very few of its businesses are geared to tourists; instead, they are dedicated to serving the community's needs. These businesses include Chinese video stores, beauty salons, sidewalk shacks purveying grilled meats and dumplings, and bakeries whose wedding cakes are topped with Asian bride-and-groom figurines.

☕ **Take a Break** For lunch, treat yourself to **dim sum** (see box below). Every day from 8am to about 4pm, two huge restaurants—the **Golden Unicorn** at 18 East Broadway (☎ 212/941-0911) and the **Nice Restaurant** at 35 East Broadway (☎ 212/406-9510)—draw large, hungry crowds. The Golden Unicorn's walkie-talkie–wielding hostess directs incoming diners to the restaurant's second- and third-floor dining rooms; in the Nice Restaurant, the lobby has several tanks full of carp and sea bass. In both restaurants, you'll usually be seated with other parties around a huge banquet table. Once settled, you'll see that a distinctly celebratory spirit pervades in the places; the Chinese families dining here often seem to have three or four generations represented. Help yourself: You can afford to take some risks because everything costs just $2 to $4 (prices at Nice are a tad lower than those at the Golden Unicorn). Though servers seldom speak much English, fellow Chinese diners or inveterate dim summers at your table might be able to offer some helpful tips.

Dim Sum

Dim sum is Cantonese for "dot your heart," and a dim sum meal consists of one small gastronomic delight after another. Simply choose what looks appealing from the steaming carts that servers wheel around to your table. Dim sum usually involves more than 100 appetizer-sized items such as steamed leek dumplings, deep-fried minced shrimp rolls wrapped in bacon, sweet doughy buns filled with tangy morsels of barbecued pork, deep-fried shrimp, beef ribs with black pepper sauce, and honey roast pork rolled in steamed noodles. Dessert dim sum may include orange pudding, egg custard rolls covered with shredded coconut, and sweet lotus-seed sesame balls.

Backtrack to Chatham Square. At the Bowery, on the square, a narrow, crooked street bears off to the northwest (in the general direction of Canal St.). This street is:

8. **Doyers Street,** which along with Pell Street and the lower end of Mott Street formed the original Chinatown. Doyers Street was the backdrop for much of the neighborhood's unhappy early history.

Chinatown's "bachelor society," which existed from 1882 to 1943 (when some provisions of the Exclusion Act were repealed), was a place of grimly limited opportunity and deep poverty. There were 27 men to every woman in the neighborhood. These men were prohibited from competing with whites for work, hemmed into Chinatown by the language barrier, and living under the risk of beatings if they strayed from the 3-block ghetto. Under these harsh conditions, working in the laundry industry was one of the best ways to eke out a living.

Crime compounded the neighborhood's misery. The Chinese moved into the northern end of an area that for 40 years had been a sprawling morass of saloons, gambling dens, and squalid tenements extending from Chatham Square all the way to the waterfront. Prostitution flourished (out of desperation, many Chinese men lived with, or even married, white prostitutes), and opium dens sprang up. The Chinese Consolidated Benevolent Association (CCBA) acted as de facto government, but the real power resided in the *tongs,* "protection societies" (much like the Mafia) involved in racketeering and gambling. There are still tong-controlled gaming dens in Chinatown, still whispers of intimidation, and an occasional outbreak of gang-related violence.

The post office, located a few paces up Doyers Street on your right, occupies the site of the old Chatham Club, one of the uproarious music halls that surrounded Chatham Square a century ago. The clubs boasted singing waiters, accompanied by a tinny piano, who would entertain the clientele with sentimental ballads. Izzy Baline and Al Yoelson sang at the Chatham and other clubs on Doyers; later, in tonier surroundings, they became better known as Irving Berlin and Al Jolson.

By the 1920s, the sharp bend in Doyers Street had acquired its reputation as the infamous:

9. **"Bloody Angle."** The first two tongs to rise in Chinatown, the On Leong and the Hip Sing, engaged in a fierce turf struggle in Chinatown that dragged on for almost 40 years. Both organizations had large standing armies of henchmen, and the worst of the continual bloodshed occurred here. The crooked street lent itself to ambush, and assassins could usually make a fast escape by ducking through the old Chinese Theatre, which stood at the elbow of the street that the Viet-Nam restaurant now occupies. At the turn of the 20th century, Bloody Angle was the site of more murders than anywhere else in the United States.

At the end of Doyers Street is Pell Street, another short, narrow thoroughfare lined with restaurants. Pell Street has also changed little over the years. At no. 16 is the unobtrusive entryway to the headquarters of the organization that has dominated Pell and Doyers streets for 100 years, the Hip Sing tong; the gold lettering above the door symbolizes growth and prosperity.

Leaving the dark side of the neighborhood's history behind, turn left on Pell Street down to its intersection with:

10. **Mott Street,** the heart of old Chinatown. Mott Street is the epicenter of the boisterous Chinese New Year celebrations that begin with the first full moon after January 21. Red and gold streamers festoon every shop window, and the street fills with parades complete with gyrating dragon dancers and the nonstop thunder of firecrackers.

The shops that line Mott Street are a diverse bunch, and their collective stock gives you the chance to bring a piece of Chinatown back home. Just around the corner to your left is one such store:

11. **Quong Yuen Shing & Company** at 32 Mott St. The oldest store in Chinatown, Quong Yuen Shing celebrated its 110th birthday in 2001. It has changed remarkably little. The tin ceiling, hanging scales, and decorative panels in back above the ornately decorated counter (over which Chinese herbal medicines were once dispensed) all keep

the place looking just as it did in the 1890s. Along with sandalwood fans, tea, mah-jongg sets, ceramic bowls and vases, and seeds for Chinese vegetables, the store still sells merchandise that it has been stocking for a century. One such item is silk handkerchiefs, which Chinatown laundries used to buy and pass on to their best customers at Christmastime.

Continue along Mott Street and cross to the:

12. **Sinotique** at 19a Mott St. Inside this refined, decidedly upscale shop you'll find beautiful, high-quality Chinese antiques, crafts, and collectibles. On a recent visit, the offerings included rosewood and teak cabinets with delicate hand-carved ornamentation; pottery ranging from unglazed pieces created in the 2nd millennium B.C. to works from the Ching dynasty (1644–1912); exquisite carved bamboo birdcages from southern China (ask them to explain the traditional bird-keeping hobby common among old Chinese men); Chinese country furniture; Tibetan, Chinese, and Mongolian rugs; hand-wrought mounted bronze gongs; and jewelry.

Backtrack up Mott to cross tiny Mosco Street, and you'll be in front of the:

13 **Church of the Transfiguration** at 25–29 Mott St. This Georgian stone church was built in 1801; the spire was added in the 1860s. Originally consecrated as the English Lutheran First Church of Zion, the church has been a veritable chameleon, always reflecting the changing image of the neighborhood. It was first created as a house of worship for English Lutherans. It then morphed into a church for the newly arrived Irish Catholics, and later, in the 1880s, became a house of worship for Italian Catholics. Nowadays its services are in Cantonese and Mandarin, and the church is the focal point of New York's Chinese Roman Catholic community. Transfiguration remains true to its long heritage as a mission house, continuing to offer English classes and other services that help its members find their way into the American mainstream.

Take a Break Just beyond Pell Street is the **New Lung Fong Bakery** at 41 Mott St. (☎ 212/233-7447), offering an array of sweet treats such as red-bean cakes, black-bean doughnuts, lotus seed–moon cake custard tarts, chestnut buns, cream buns, melon cakes, and mixed-nut pies. Sitting in Lung Fong's unadorned cafe section, you can relax with a cup of tea or very good coffee and *yum cha*—that's Chinese for hanging out, talking, and drinking in a cafe.

Next door is the new **Aji Ichiban,** 37 Mott St. (☎ 212/233-7650; www.ajiichiban-usa.com), a self-proclaimed "munchies paradise" that looks innocuously like any bulk candy store you'd see in the mall—until you start perusing the English translations of what's in each bin. Candy-coated chocolates that look like decorative pebbles, shriveled fruits of the sorts you didn't even know could be dried, and dozens of licorices mixed in among bins for snack-sized morsels of such things as dried squid. We dare to close your eyes and make a selection.

Continue north on Mott. On the right at 42 Mott St. is the:

14. **Ming Fay Book Store.** An eclectic store stocked with everything from art/school supplies and toys to Chinese calendars, newspapers, comics, pinup magazines, and books, Ming Fay also carries a selection of English-language books on Chinese subjects. Here is a sampling of titles: *Chinese Astrology, The Bruce Lee Story, The Book of Tea, The Dictionary of Traditional Chinese Medicine,* and *The Living Buddha.*

A little farther up Mott at no. 62 is the headquarters of the:

15. **Chinese Consolidated Benevolent Association (CCBA).** Until recently, this association functioned as the working government of Chinatown, helping new immigrants find jobs and housing, funneling capital into neighborhood businesses, offering English classes to children and adults, providing services to the elderly, and even operating criminal courts. Although its influence has waned somewhat, it is still a major social and political force in Chinatown and is the voice of New York's pro-Taiwan community. Also located in the building is the Chinese School, which since 1915 has been working to

keep Chinese traditions and language alive, long a primary concern of the CCBA.

Two doors down is the:

16. **Eastern States Buddhist Temple of America.**
Quiet and suffused with incense and the smell of cooking oil (they use it ritualistically), this storefront shrine has been here for years and serves as something of a social center; usually a number of elderly ladies are sitting in the chairs and benches that line the wall. Enter, light a joss stick, and offer a prayer to Kuan-yin, the Chinese goddess of mercy. Or perhaps you'd rather supplicate the Four-Faced Buddha for good luck in business (money will come from all directions, hence the four faces). You can also buy a fortune here, in English, for a dollar.

Across the street and up at the corner of Mott and Canal streets (83–85 Mott), behind a stately facade featuring balconies and a pagoda roof, is the headquarters of the **Chinese Merchants Association,** better known as the **On Leong** tong. Chinatown's oldest tong is still one of its most prominent neighborhood organizations.

Make a left onto Canal Street, where a steady stream of shoppers will no doubt be passing in and out of:

17. **Kam Man Food Inc.** at 200 Canal St. This quintessential Chinese supermarket is a fascinating browse. To your right as you enter is a selection of elaborately packaged teas and elixirs laced with ginseng and other mainstays of Chinese pharmacopoeia. These products include tzepao sanpien extract (which promises greater potency to men), heart tonics, smoking cessation and slimming teas, deer-tail extract, edible bird's nests, tiger liniment, and royal jelly. Many of these products claim to cure a wide variety of ailments. *Bu tian su,* for example, is supposedly good for memory loss, insomnia, an aching back, or lumbago, among other things. Just beyond this collection is a counter displaying myriad varieties of ginseng. Walk toward the rear of the store, and you'll find packages of pork buns ready for the steamer, quail eggs, dried seafood, exotic mushrooms, sauces ranging from oyster to black-bean garlic, a butcher section, and much more. Downstairs, the kitchenware department offers everything from woks to tea sets and a

counter for fancy chopsticks, roasted seaweed, and oodles of noodles. Pick up some essence of *tienchi* flowers, a purported remedy for pimples, dizziness, hot temper, grinding of teeth, and emotional inquietude.

Turn left onto Mulberry Street (another thoroughfare lined with emporia that make for great browsing and window shopping) to visit the:

18. **Museum of Chinese in America,** 70 Mulberry St. (☎ 212/619-4785; www.moca-nyc.org). In the forward-looking, upwardly mobile climate of today's Chinatown, it's tough to think about the cruel hardships that the first generations of Chinese in New York suffered. This museum, founded in 1980, documents the history and culture of Chinese in America from the early 1800s to the present. An adjoining gallery stages exhibitions of works by Chinese artists and photographers; the museum also includes a gift/bookstore. Hours are noon to 5pm on Tuesday, Wednesday, Thursday, and Saturday; the museum charges a small admission.

Opening off to the southwest on the other side of Mulberry Street is:

19. **Columbus Park.** Open public spaces are in short supply on the Lower East Side, and dingy but lively Columbus Park is popular with Chinatown residents both young and old. In this park, older Chinese women play cards for dimes or have their fortunes told while Chinese men gamble over checkers. The park lies where a huddle of decrepit tenements known as Mulberry Bend once stood. In the last quarter of the 19th century, Mulberry Bend was New York's worst slum, as evinced by the frightening nomenclature it acquired—the filthy tenements went by names such as Bone Alley, Kerosene Row, and Bandits' Roost. Such brawling street gangs as the Dead Rabbits, Plug Uglies, and Whyos were the powers of Mulberry Bend, and police ventured into the area only in platoons of 10 or more.

Mulberry Bend remained New York's disgrace until social reformer Jacob Riis managed to stir up public rage to the point where city officials were obliged to raze the slum between 1892 and 1894. For the last century, Riis's vision of a clean place for neighborhood children to play has been a reality: there's a big playground, and games of basketball, baseball, or hockey are almost always in progress.

At the southern end of the park, make a left turn onto Worth Street, and you'll soon be back at Chatham Square. Up ahead on your right on the traffic island is the:

20. **Kimlau War Memorial,** built in 1962 to honor the Chinese Americans who gave their lives while serving in the U.S. armed forces. Chinatown's extraordinary contribution to the American war effort in World War II—40% of the neighborhood's population served in the military—was a major factor in the annulment of the Chinese Exclusion Act and other anti-Chinese legislation.

St. James Place, which extends south from Chatham Square, is the site of the:

21. **First Shearith Israel Graveyard,** a burial ground for Sephardic Jews who immigrated to New York in the mid–17th century. The 1683 stone of Benjamin Bueno de Mesquita (still legible) is the oldest in the city; the cemetery remained active until 1828 and features the graves of a number of soldiers who died during the American Revolution.

Also buried here, in 1733, is Rachel Rodriguez Marques, an ancestor of New York stockbroker, politico, and college benefactor Bernard Baruch (who paid for the improvement of the site in the 1950s). The gate is usually locked, but you can peer through the fence.

Backtrack on St. James Place, and turn right onto Oliver Street. On the northeast corner of Oliver and Henry streets is the:

22. **Mariner's Temple.** This Greek Revival brownstone church, with a portico entranceway fronted by two massive Ionic columns, was built in 1844. Today a Baptist church serving a mixed Chinese, African American, and Latino congregation, the Mariner's Temple originally catered to the sea captains, dockworkers, and sailors of the sprawling maritime community that dominated the waterfront along the East River in the 19th century.

Turn left onto Henry Street. Two blocks east, on the corner of Henry and Market streets, is the:

23. **First Chinese Presbyterian Church,** which shares a place in neighborhood history with the Mariner's Temple. Built in 1819 on the outskirts of the Cherry Hill section (which after the Revolutionary War was New York's poshest neighborhood and the site of the nation's first presidential mansion), this Georgian-style house of worship was originally named the Northeast Dutch Reformed Church. It was renamed the Church of Sea and Land during the mid–19th century, when the East River waterfront had become rife with cutthroat saloons, dance halls, and "crimps"—lodging houses that often took advantage of their sailor patrons by robbing them or even shanghaiing them aboard outgoing ships. Mission houses such as the Mariner's Temple and the Church of Sea and Land were often the only place to which beleaguered seafarers and immigrants could turn for help. Today, the church continues to assist the immigrants who arrive in Chinatown in droves every year.

Turn left and follow Market Street to bustling East Broadway and turn right. Believe it or not, the dim, noisy area below the Manhattan Bridge is a commercial hot spot of Chinatown. On your left is the modest:

24. **East Broadway Mall.** The stores here cater entirely to Chinese shoppers and include a newsstand at which you'll be lucky to spot a word of English, a Chinese pop music shop, two Chinese-language video stores, several beauty salons and cosmetics shops selling products you won't find in your average beauty store, and Ho's Ginseng Co., where you can get something to cool down your blood (or warm it up). The mall's centerpiece is a glitzy upstairs restaurant, the Triple Eight Palace.

Continue along East Broadway, and you'll soon cross Pike Street. Pike is an unofficial divider between the established area of Chinatown and an expanding area that's been termed:

25. **Chinatown's "Wild West"** by journalist Gwen Kinkead in her book *Chinatown: A Portrait of a Closed*

Society (HarperCollins, 1992). Asians have been flooding into New York City ever since U.S. immigration laws were liberalized in 1965. The great majority of them hail from the People's Republic of China, and most of these new immigrants come from Fujian Province, often via Hong Kong or Taiwan. These new arrivals have almost completely replaced the old immigrant residents of the Lower East Side, the Jews. Emblematic of the changing makeup in the neighborhood is the Sons of Israel Kalwarie Synagogue, located on Pike Street to the right of East Broadway—it's now a Buddhist association.

Walk down East Broadway to Rutgers Street (where you'll find the entrance to the subway's East Broadway F-line stop). The Chinatown you'll pass on your way may not have curio shops or pagoda roofs, but the barber shops, fish markets, and newsstands do a brisk business. All throughout this neighborhood, you'll see hectic commerce, hardworking laborers, and schoolchildren, and you can sense the buzz of a neighborhood where many people are working to leave these gritty tenement streets and make their way into the mainstream, just as people on the Lower East Side have been doing for more than a century.

The Jewish Lower East Side

Start: Bialystoker Synagogue, 7 Bialystoker Place.

Subway: Take the F train to Delancey Street or the J, M, or Z to Essex Street.

Finish: Russ and Daughters, 179 Houston St.

Time: 3½ to 4 hours if you do all the tours.

Best Time: Sundays, when you can tour the Eldridge Street Synagogue (stop 6) and see Orchard Street in full form. If you begin around 9:30am, you'll also get a chance to look inside Bialystoker Synagogue (stop 1). *Note:* Because tours of the highly recommended Lower East Side Tenement Museum sometimes fill up on Sundays, you might want to stop there earlier in the day (it opens at 11am) and pick up tickets; see details below (stop 11).

Worst Time: Saturdays and Jewish holidays (when almost everything is closed) and Friday afternoons (when stores close early).

T he Lower East Side (www.lowereastsideny.com) has always been one of New York's most colorful neighborhoods. More than 23 million Europeans immigrated to American shores between 1880 and 1919, seeking escape from famine, poverty, and religious persecution. About 1.5 million Jews, many of them fleeing Russian pogroms, wound up in ramshackle tenements here. They scratched out meager livings peddling wares on Orchard Street or working dawn to dusk in garment center sweatshops. By 1920, some 500 synagogues and religious schools (Talmud Torahs) dotted the area. Though the garment center has moved uptown and the ethnic mix of the Lower East Side is different today, Orchard Street, the area's primary shopping artery, and its immediate surroundings remain a largely Orthodox Jewish enclave. The area is rich in Jewish history; 80% of today's American Jews are descendants of immigrants who once lived on these streets. Today, more Jews—almost two million—live in New York City than anywhere else in the world outside of Israel.

Food note: This tour has great noshing (a Yiddish word for snacking) along the way, so you can use it as an eating tour as well as a walking tour.

• • • • • • • • • • • • • • • •

Starting out **Ratner's Dairy Restaurant,** 138 Delancey St. between Norfolk and Suffolk streets (☎ **212/677-5588**), is the oldest Jewish dairy restaurant in the city. People have been coming here since 1905 (first to Grand St., then, since 1917, to the present location) to feast on cheese and berry blintzes smothered in sour cream, kreplach (boiled dumplings filled with cheese or meat), gefilte fish (the way Grandma used to make it), whitefish salad, potato latkes, and matzo *brei* (matzo mixed with egg and then fried).

Ratner's has always been popular with New York politicos wooing the Jewish vote. Former Gov. Nelson Rockefeller always ate here the night before elections; he said it was good luck. During the 1989 Democratic mayoral primary, rival candidates David Dinkins and Ed Koch were surprised to run into each other at breakfast one morning; they civilly shook hands and proceeded to devour bagels and lox.

The Jewish Lower East Side

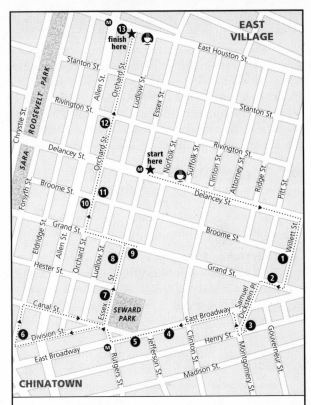

1 Bialystoker Synagogue

2 Abrons Arts Center/Harry De Jur Playhouse

3 The Henry Street Settlement

4 Educational Alliance (the David Sarnoff Building)

5 Forward Building

6 Eldridge Street Synagogue

7 Weinfeld's Skull Cap Mfg.

8 Hebrew Religious Articles

9 Kossar's Bialys

10 Guss Pickles

11 Lower East Side Tenement Museum

12 Orchard Street

13 Russ and Daughters

Ⓜ Subway
☕ Take a Break

0   0.1 mile

0   100 meters

All breads and cakes are baked on the premises. A basket of scrumptious onion rolls accompanies every meal, and the desserts are great (try the strawberry cheesecake or chocolate cream pie). Sadly, Ratner's is now open only on Sundays from 8am to 8pm, with its after-dark alter ego **The Lansky Lounge** taking over daily from around 6pm until 4 or 5am (it's closed on Sat from mid-May though early Oct). Rumor has it the whole shebang is up for sale, though, so call ahead before planning to breakfast here.

From Ratner's, cross Delancey Street; turn left and walk down the south side of the street for a few blocks, around to the right of the bridge ramp. Take a right onto Bialystoker Place/Willett Street. On the right, just past Broome Street, is the:

1. **Bialystoker Synagogue,** 7 Bialystoker Place (Willett St.). Occupying a converted 1826 Federal-style fieldstone church, this beautiful Orthodox *landsmanschaft shul* (synagogue of countrymen) was purchased in 1905 by an immigrant congregation from Bialystok (then a town in Russia; today, because of changing borders, in Poland). The congregation itself was organized in 1878, and in honor of its 100th anniversary, Willett Street was renamed Bialystoker Place in 1978. Enter via the downstairs steps below the main doors. The temple's interior walls and ceiling are ornately painted with Moorish motifs, zodiac signs (which are found in Jewish cabala writings), and biblical scenes such as the Wailing Wall and the burial place of Rachel. The elaborate gold-leafed ark (which contains the Torahs) was designed in Italy. Look up at the glittering crystal chandeliers, which hang from a ceiling painted as a blue sky with fluffy white clouds.

Bialystoker Synagogue is open daily (except for Sat, the Jewish sabbath) until about 10:30am (sometimes later) and evenings (except for Fri) from 6:30 to 8pm; if you're going at another time, you can call a day or two ahead (☎ 212/475-0165) to arrange admission.

Continue up Willett Street and make a right onto Grand Street. The modern, curvilinear brick building on your right is the modern extension of the:

Kid-Friendly Experiences

- Slurping down a pickle at Guss Pickles (stop 10)
- Taking the kid-targeted Confino Apartment tour at the Lower East Side Tenement Museum (stop 11— call for tour reservations)
- Bargain-hunting on Orchard Street (stop 12)

2. **Abrons Arts Center/Harry De Jur Playhouse,** 466 Grand St. (☎ **212/598-0400;** www.henrystreet.org). Founded by sisters Alice and Irene Lewisohn in 1915 to stage productions by the Henry Street Settlement's youth dramatic groups, this renowned center went on to present premieres of S. Ansky's *The Dybbuk* (attended by authors Edna Ferber and Willa Cather) and James Joyce's *Exiles,* along with plays by George Bernard Shaw, Havelock Ellis, Anton Chekhov, Scholem Asch, and Eugene O'Neill. It remains a vital performance space and cultural center, offering a comprehensive schedule of dance, theater, music, art exhibits, classes, and workshops. Pick up an events schedule while you're here. Behind this modern extension is the center's original core: a three-story Georgian Revival building.

   Cross Grand and head left down Samuel Dickstein Plaza. After crossing East Broadway, the plaza spills into the intersection of Henry and Montgomery streets. Take a sharp left onto Henry Street, and immediately on your left is:

3. **The Henry Street Settlement,** 263–267 Henry St. Called to tend a patient on Ludlow Street in 1892, 25-year-old German-Jewish nurse Lillian Wald was appalled at the squalor of tenement life. She moved downtown in order to study the living conditions in the Jewish ghetto and established a district nursing service on Henry Street in 1893. Two years later, the service evolved into the Henry Street Settlement, one of America's first social agencies. It offered job training, educational facilities, summer camps for children, concerts, and plays.

Wald dedicated her life to helping the indigent of the Lower East Side fight disease, malnutrition, and ignorance, and the "house on Henry Street" initiated progressive social legislation, including child labor laws. Social reformer Jacob Riis said of Lillian Wald, "From the very start, the poor became 'her people.' She took them to her heart, and they quickly gave her unstinted love and trust." Years ago, you might have seen Jane Addams, Albert Einstein, or Eleanor Roosevelt discussing vital social issues in the dining room. President Bill Clinton visited during his 1992 campaign. The settlement continues its good works, operating homeless shelters and numerous programs for neighborhood residents. Its three original late-Federal/Classic Revival buildings—built in 1832 (no. 265), 1908 (no. 267), and 1934 (no. 263)—are now used for administrative purposes and are designated landmarks.

Turn around and head back to the corner, where you make a right back up Montgomery Street (through the small cement park) toward the high-rise apartments, and take a left onto East Broadway. A ways down on your left is the:

4. **Educational Alliance (the David Sarnoff Building),** 197 East Broadway. "Uptown" German-Jewish philanthropists founded The Alliance in 1889 to help fellow immigrants assimilate, Americanize, and adapt to a baffling alien culture. It offered them training in English, courses in business, cultural and civic programs, legal counsel, music lessons, and athletic facilities, not to mention such hard-to-come-by amenities as hot showers and pasteurized milk for children.

Today, the Educational Alliance's programs operate out of 21 locations and serve not only Jews, but also African-, Chinese-, and Latin-American New Yorkers. A Hall of Fame on the main floor is lined with photos of notable alumni such as Eddie Cantor, David Sarnoff, Jan Peerce, Jacob Epstein, Arthur Murray, and Louise Nevelson.

Continue in the same direction. You'll notice by the signs that the old Jewish neighborhood here has given way to the ever-expanding and vibrant Chinese neighborhood, which far exceeds the traditional boundaries that maps label "Chinatown." At 175 East Broadway, you'll see the tall, old:

5. **Forward Building.** For 60 years, this building was the home of America's most prominent Yiddish newspaper, the *Forverts* (in English, *The Forward*). Founded in 1897 by a group of Russian Jewish immigrants, the *Forverts* guided thousands of Eastern European Jews through the confusing maze of American society. In the 1920s, its daily circulation reached 250,000 copies.

Lithuanian immigrant Abraham Cahan served as editor of the newspaper from its inception until his death in 1951. Under his guidance, this socialist and zealously pro-labor newspaper examined every facet of Jewish and American life. It explained American customs and social graces to greenhorns—everything from baseball to personal hygiene—and exhorted readers to learn English and educate their children. The paper also presented—along with trashy serialized romance novels—quality fiction by writers like Sholem Asch, Sholom Aleichem, I. J. Singer, and I. B. Singer. The latter Singer worked on the newspaper's staff throughout his adult life, and all of his books, which were written in Yiddish (later translated), were first published in *The Forward*.

Today the Forward building, constructed in 1912 specifically to house the paper, is a Chinese-American community center. Though the male and female figures centered on a sunburst above the door remain (they symbolize enlightenment), the flaming torches (socialist symbols) and portraits of Marx and Engels on the building's facade are obscured by Chinese signage. *The Forward* still exists today as a vital newspaper headquartered uptown. Since 1990, it has been published in English as well as in Yiddish.

In the heyday of the *Forverts,* the Chinese restaurant now occupying the corner of Rutgers Street and East Broadway was the Garden Cafeteria, a superb dairy restaurant patronized by members of the Jewish intelligentsia; Leon Trotsky frequently dined here when he was in New York.

Cross Rutgers Street and turn right up it, and then turn left on Canal Street. At Ludlow, bear left onto Division Street, cross wide Pike/Allen Street, and make a right on Eldridge Street to find the:

6. **Eldridge Street Synagogue** (Congregation K'hal Adath Jeshurun, 12–16 Eldridge St.; ☎ 212/219-0888; www.eldridgestreet.org). When this synagogue was built in 1886–88 by a congregation of Polish and Russian Jews, it was the most magnificent synagogue on the Lower East Side. It was also the first synagogue built by Eastern European immigrants, who had previously worshipped in converted churches. Designed by the Herter Brothers (interior designers for wealthy New York families like the Vanderbilts), its architectural and interior decor reflects a blend of Gothic, Romanesque, and Moorish styles. The grandiose terra-cotta and brick facade is highly symbolic: Its cluster of five small windows represent the five books of Moses, the 12 roundels of the rose window symbolize the 12 tribes of Israel, and so on. The greatly deteriorated, but once opulent, sanctuary was fitted out under a 70-foot central dome with an ornately carved towering walnut ark from Italy, trompe l'oeil murals, stained-glass windows, scagliola (imitation marble) columns, and Victorian glass-shaded brass chandeliers.

The congregation flourished for several decades, but as wealthy members moved away and quota laws of the 1920s slowed immigration to a trickle, funds became short and the building deteriorated. By the 1940s, the main sanctuary was in such bad repair that it was boarded up. Not until the 1970s did urban preservationists and historians begin taking an interest in the building. The Eldridge Street Project, founded in 1986, is now restoring the building as an active synagogue and Jewish heritage center. The synagogue currently has a small Orthodox congregation.

Visitors can pop in for a look for a buck, or take 1-hour tours every Sunday on the hour from 11am to 4pm, Tuesday and Thursday at 11:30am and 2:30pm. Admission is charged (it goes toward the renovation). While you're here, inquire about the synagogue's many programs and lectures.

From the synagogue, continue up Eldridge Street and make your first right on Canal Street (no road sign). After a few blocks, take a left on Essex Street, where you'll find many fascinating little shops carrying Judaica, kosher foods, and religious articles.

7. **Weinfeld's Skull Cap Mfg.,** at 19 Essex St., is a century-old yarmulke factory run by succeeding generations of Weinfelds. *Yarmulkes* are small skullcaps worn by Jewish men in synagogue (and worn all day every day by many Orthodox Jews). The factory also makes *tallith* (fringed prayer shawls worn by men during Jewish religious services), prayer book bags, and tallith bags.

Continue uptown to:

8. **Hebrew Religious Articles,** 45 Essex St. (☎ 212/ 674-1770). This shop has been here for more than 50 years. Its shelves and display cases are cluttered with Jewish books, ritual phylacteries (leather cases containing Scripture passages, which are worn by Jewish men during weekday morning prayer) and shawls, sacred scrolls, commentaries on the Torah, menorahs, antique Judaica, electric memorial candles, seder plates, mezuzahs, yarmulkes, cantorial and Yiddish recordings, and a marvelous collection of turn-of-the-20th-century Eastern European postcards.

Make a right on Grand Street to find:

9. **Kossar's Bialys,** 367 Grand St., where you can watch bakers making bialys, bagels, and *bulkas* (long bialylike rolls). *Bialys* (round rolls with a dimple in the middle) were invented by bakers from the Polish town of Bialystok, and this shop has been making delicious ones since the turn of the 20th century.

Backtrack west along Grand Street, crossing Essex, and make a right onto Orchard Street. A bit up the block you'll come across the new location for:

10. **Guss Pickles** (better known as Guss Pickle Products), 85–87 Orchard St. (☎ 800/252-GUSS or 516/642-2634), which at its original location on Essex Street (the greedy landlord forced them out in 2002) was featured in

the movie *Crossing Delancey.* You'll smell the shop's briny aroma halfway down the street. Guss Pickle Products originated in 1910, and it's now run by its fourth generation. The giant plastic barrels that line the sidewalk out front are filled with sours, half sours, hot pickles, pickled tomatoes, olives, sauerkraut, horseradish, and other delicacies. Everything is made on the premises. Buy a delicious pickle to eat on the street, or purchase a jarful. It's open Sunday to Thursday 9am to 6pm and Friday 9am to 4pm.

Continue up to the corner of Broome, where you'll come to the orientation center for the:

11. **Lower East Side Tenement Museum,** 90 Orchard St. (☎ 212/431-0233; www.tenement.org). Conceived as a monument to the experience of "urban pioneers" in America, this unique facility documents the lives of immigrant residents in an 1863 six-story, 22-apartment tenement: 97 Orchard St., accessible only via the highly recommended guided tours. The tour is bookable, for a fee, at ☎ 800/965-4827 or www.ticketweb.com; Sunday tours cannot be booked in advance.

The orientation center/gift shop is where you buy tour tickets and can view a 28-minute orientation video. Also on display here are Depression-era photographs of tenement life by Hungarian-born WPA artist Arnold Eagle and some of the 1,500 objects found in nooks and crannies of the building.

The guided tours (there are three to choose from) give a thorough history, but to whet your appetite, here are a few quick facts about the building: Up to 10,000 people from 20 different countries lived at 97 Orchard over a period of 72 years (the landlord sealed the building in 1935 so he wouldn't have to bring it up to code under the new housing laws, inadvertently creating the perfect time capsule). These immigrants probably would have been astonished to hear that their crowded building of cold, cramped, airless apartments would one day be listed on the National Register of Historic Landmarks. It was reopened in 1988.

Residents lived (and often worked, sewing piecework for garment manufacturers or taking in laundry) in three-room apartments with a total area of just 325 square feet. Scant light trickled through windows at distant ends of railroad flats, and the only heat came from the coal- or wood-burning cooking stove. Large families, often supplemented by boarders for extra cash, lived in such dwellings without running water (until the 1890s it had to be fetched from a backyard pump and hauled upstairs). Other modern conveniences that tenants had to do without included indoor plumbing (until plumbing was installed at the turn of the century, chamber pots served as toilets, and slops had to be carried to privies in the backyard; after that, there were toilets in the hall) and electricity (which may not have been installed until the 1920s). Bed legs were often placed in cans of kerosene, which, though it created a fire hazard, discouraged bedbugs.

Lucas Glockner, the German immigrant who built the place, was unhampered by building codes; few existed at the time, and the ones that did were not enforced. By 1915, as many as 18 people sometimes occupied one apartment, sleeping in shifts. In such unhealthy conditions, 40% of the babies born here died, and disease was rampant. The museum has re-created two apartments based on records, letters, and the memories of people who once lived here as children, and it is currently re-creating a third.

The museum is open daily 11am to 5pm. There is an admission fee for the excellent hour-long tenement tours, which leave every 20 to 30 minutes on Tuesday to Friday from 1 to 4pm, and on weekends from 11am to 4:30pm (sometimes also Mon in summer). Pick up a schedule of the museum's weekend neighborhood tours for future excursions, including the kids-oriented **Confino Apartment tour,** in which a costumed actress re-creates the life of a teenage tenement resident by telling her story and answering questions.

Continue up the block, crossing Delancey Street, to enter the shop-lined stretch of:

12. **Orchard Street.** It's hard to imagine, but Orchard Street was named for the orchards of an 18th-century farm at this location owned by James Delancey, lieutenant governor of the British province of New York (Delancey St. is named for him). In the 19th century, this street was a vast outdoor marketplace lined with rows of pushcarts.

Today, pushcarts have been replaced by stores, though much of the merchandise is still displayed outside on racks. You can save up to 50% over uptown department stores here, and many shop owners are willing to haggle over prices. However, don't expect polite service. On Sundays the street is so jammed with shoppers that it is closed to vehicular traffic between Delancey and Houston streets. But Orchard Street on Sunday is a phenomenon you must experience at least once. Come back to do serious shopping on a weekday when you have the stores to yourself.

Continue north on Orchard Street, turning left on Houston Street. Your last stop is:

13. **Russ and Daughters,** 179 East Houston St. (☎ 212/ 475-4880). Joel and Bella Russ began selling food from a pushcart in 1911. Their operation evolved into one of New York's most famous appetizer stores, which is now run by their grandson, Mark Federman. At this final stop on the tour, you can stock up on Nova lox, creamed or schmaltz herring, whitefish salad, gefilte fish, halvah, and other Jewish delicacies, and take a little of the Lower East Side home with you.

Winding Down Katz's Delicatessen, 205 East Houston St. at Ludlow Street (☎ 212/254-2246), is a classic New York deli that's been in business at this location since 1889. The interior is little changed from those days. Even the World War II sign reading "Send a salami to your boy in the Army" is still intact. Katz's was the setting for Meg Ryan's famous faked orgasm scene in the movie *When Harry Met Sally*.

"She didn't really fake it," says owner Fred Austin, "it was the food." Between takes, costar Billy Crystal, a great Katz's fan, wolfed down a dozen corned beef sandwiches, supplemented with hot dogs, cherry peppers, and pickles. Note the photographs of Katz's in the old days and its famous patrons hanging in the window and on the blond wood walls; everyone from Jackie Mason to Houdini to Bill Clinton has eaten here. Order a pastrami or corned beef sandwich on rye (it's stuffed with about ¾ pound of meat), a potato knish, and a New York egg cream. Current owner Austin took the place over from the Katz family about a decade ago, but he hasn't changed a thing, not even the archetypal surly Jewish waiter service. "If anyone's nice to a customer, I want to hear about it," he says. There's cafeteria and waiter service. Katz's is open Sunday to Wednesday 8am to 10pm, Thursday 8am to 11pm, and Friday and Saturday 8am to midnight.

SoHo

Start: Broadway and Prince Street.

Subway: Take the N or R train to Prince Street.

Finish: West Broadway, just below Spring Street.

Time: Anywhere from 3 to 5 hours, depending on how long you spend browsing galleries, museums, and shops.

Best Time: Start around 10:30am, because most galleries are open 11am to 5pm (and the breakfast stop is one of the best in the city). Return in the evening for an opening to experience the art scene at its schmooziest.

Worst Time: Sunday and Monday, when almost all galleries and most museums are closed; mid-July to early September, when many galleries are closed or open only by appointment.

Everyone has a different image that springs to mind when they hear the name New York. *Seinfeld* fans picture the Upper West Side, corporate types imagine hitting it big on Wall Street, literary aficionados and ex-hippies have Greenwich Village flashbacks, and latter-day bohemians conjure up the East Village. I grew up with a painter for a father and he frequently took me to his New York, the multihued nucleus of the international art world. As a result, my eternal image of the Big Apple is SoHo.

SoHo

GREENWICH VILLAGE

Houston St.

finish here ★

start here ★

Cleveland Pl.

Kenmare St.

Grand St.

TRIBECA

| 0 | 0.1 mile |
| 0 | 100 meters |

Ⓜ Subway
☕ Take a Break

1 Lennon, Weinberg/
   Cavin-Morris
2 Singer Building/
   Kate's Paperie
3 Prada
4 The New Museum of
   Contemporary Art
5 American Primitive Gallery
6 Eileen's Special Cheesecake
7 Haughwout Building
8 St. Nicholas Hotel
9 101 Spring Street
10 105 Mercer Street
11 The Enchanted Forest
12 Gourmet Garage
13 Yohji Yamamoto
14 Roland Feldman Fine Arts
15 Pearl Paint
16 Greene Street
17 91-93 Grand Street
18 Artists Space
19 Jack Tilton Gallery
20 Gunther Building
21 "King of Greene Street"
22 agnes b. homme
23 Richard Haas Mural
24 Fanelli's Café
25 Phyllis Kind Gallery
26 Moss
27 The Metropolitan Museum
   of Art Shop
28 Harriet Love
29 The DIA Center for the Arts
30 Tony Shafrazi
31 Cynthia Rowley/c.i.t.e.
32 Brooke Alexander Editions
33 The Drawing Center
34 American Fine Arts, Co.
35 Anthropologie/O.K. Harris
36 *The Broken Kilometer*
37 Nancy Hoffman
38 Vesuvio Bakery
39 Louis K. Meisel Gallery

Traditional SoHo, incorporating the area south (So) of Houston (Ho) Street and north of Canal Street and bounded by Broadway and West Broadway, is roughly 1 square mile. In the early 19th century, it was a run-down neighborhood lost between lower Manhattan and the mansions of uptown. Drygoods merchants and emerging manufacturing companies moved in and filled the area with warehouses that incorporated the latest in cost-cutting building technology: cast-iron facades.

Prefabricated facades of cast iron represented a simple and cheap way to garnish a structure with a face that was ornate, costly looking, and stylish (which at first meant classically inspired Italian Renaissance style and later meant French architectural style). The facades were mass produced in sections, and you could order one to fit your building from a catalog and quickly assemble and bolt it to a building's frame. You could paint it any color you wished, move it to a new building if need be, and even recycle it by melting it down and recasting it when new tastes in architecture arose. The light frames made heavy outer walls unnecessary and allowed the builders to fill up the street frontage with large windows instead, prefacing the skyscraper style. By 1962, the partially abandoned neighborhood was going to be razed to put in a highway, but architecture buffs and residents fought back, and by 1973, SoHo was declared by the city to be a historic district.

In the 1950s and '60s, artists, who were attracted by the low costs and huge, light-filled spaces, began renting unused floors of these warehouses (illegally, because the area wasn't zoned for residential use) and setting up studios with a bed and a hot plate in the corner. By the 1970s, zoning restrictions had changed, and more artists flooded the area. With so much art being produced, it was only natural that new art dealers, in a profession that formerly inhabited only the posh neighborhoods of Uptown, began to open up shops in SoHo. These dealers championed the neighborhood's emerging art stars while turning a nice profit at the same time. Established galleries from Uptown soon followed suit, and SoHo became the mecca of the contemporary art world in the late '70s and early '80s. Thrift stores and funky boutiques opened, abandoned shop fronts were filled with inexpensive diners, and, inevitably, the yuppies soon caught wind of it all.

In the 1980s, young professionals living in Manhattan's cramped, expensive apartments and co-ops saw the chance both to be hip and to get a huge pad at a low cost by moving into converted SoHo lofts. They swarmed into the neighborhood, with pricey boutiques trailing along behind. Sandwich shops like Dean and Deluca were transformed into fine food emporia. These new arrivals quickly drove the rents up into the stratosphere and were almost universally resented by SoHo's artist community, even though some new inhabitants did buy art as decoration for their empty wall space. It wasn't long before artists, even those of the nonstarving persuasion, couldn't afford to move in, and long-established SoHo residents found their own rents escalating.

In the 1990s, tourists quickly followed in the yuppies' wake, and chain stores and other paeans to mass tourism started popping up.

With the turn of the 21st century, SoHo has become a neighborhood with a split personality. An artistic and hip air remains despite overexposure. Some struggling artists' co-op exhibition spaces, funky shops, and cheap cafes still fill the streets, and many artists continue to create in their converted apartment/studios behind historic cast-iron facades.

But the hype has changed SoHo forever, from heavily commercial fine art "galleries" (though if you ask me, a room full of art with price tags is not enough to make a true gallery) and an ever-speeding influx of chillingly expensive brand-name high fashion boutiques, to overpriced bistros and converted lofts.

This is probably *not* the SoHo you came to see. Parts of SoHo are like a huge outdoor high-end shopping mall that happens to have some lovely cast iron facades, cobblestone streets, and the ghosts of a few art galleries. Just a few years ago the galleries here provided a collective museum of the best that the international contemporary art world had to offer, but this has changed as galleries close and move out. If you want to see the hottest contemporary art, don't bother with SoHo; head north to Chelsea or across the river to Williamsburg in Brooklyn.

Still, there's no neighborhood quite like SoHo, and, to me at least, there's none that so fully evokes the vibrancy, diversity, and creative energy of New York. Your walk through

SoHo takes you past the weird industrial beauty of the cast-iron age, into some of the more interesting shops and fashion outlets (these things change every few weeks, so except for some long-established ones, I'll limit myself to mentioning the big names in passing as we walk up the block that their outlets currently inhabit), and past the doors of the surviving galleries.

• • • • • • • • • • • • • • • • • •

Starting Out Dean and Deluca (☎ 212/226-6800; www.dean-deluca.com), at the southeast corner of Broadway and Prince Street, is a true New York institution. Although now expanded to multiple branches, and priced a bit out of starving-artist range, Dean and Deluca remains one of Manhattan's older and more beloved fine food shops. It started as a lunch counter serving superb sandwiches. You can still get these excellent sandwiches inside, along with a cornucopia of imported, farm-fresh, and gourmet foods, and, in the back, kitchenware. At the very least, grab a cappuccino and a pastry (or my favorite, a giant spiced ginger cookie) and sit at the bar counter facing the plate glass window to watch one of SoHo's busiest intersections and gird yourself for the gallery scene.

Dean and Deluca's storefront is under 560 Broadway, home to several galleries (the entrance is a few doors south on Broadway) including:

1. **Lennon, Weinberg** (☎ 212/941-0012). This gallery on the third floor represents many well-established contemporary artists (Chuck Connelly, Willem de Kooning, Catherine Murphy, Joan Mitchell), with leanings toward the abstract. On the fourth floor is **Cavin-Morris** (☎ 212/226-3768), which mainly shows works by self-taught, non-American artists—often museum-quality works from Africa, the Caribbean, and so-called "developing" countries around the world.

   As you exit 560 Broadway, you'll see across the street the terra-cotta facade and long, graceful arches of the:

2. **Singer Building,** designed by Ernest Flagg in 1904 as an office and warehouse for the sewing machine giant.

The 12-story facade with large glass windows and a steel frame was an architectural novelty at the time and prefigured the plate-glass walls of later 20th-century skyscrapers.

The Singer building's ground floor houses **Kate's Paperie** (☎ 212/633-0570; www.katespaperie.com), which sells paper and stationery items of the highest quality and inventiveness, along with housewares in the back. Cross Broadway to at least poke your head in for a glance at the paper geometry of the ceiling. Then cross Prince Street so you're standing on the northwest corner.

Filling the russet 19th-century building at this corner is the symbol of everything that's changed in the new SoHo. It still says "Guggenheim SoHo" on the facade, but inside it has become a:

3. **Prada** designer boutique. A year ago, on this block alone, along with the Guggenheim there was the Alternative Museum and the Museum for African Art. Now all that remains (and you gotta wonder how long they'll stick it out now that their neighbors are no longer their peers but rather Armani Exchange, Kenneth Cole, and Eddie Bauer), a few doors up Broadway at no. 583, is:

4. **The New Museum of Contemporary Art** (☎ 212/219-1222; www.newmuseum.org). In 1977, Marcia Tucker left her post as curator of the Whitney Museum on ideological grounds. The Whitney, like most museums, showcased mainly works of establishment-approved artists who were either dead or past the vital, relevant stage of their careers. Tucker founded the New Museum with no permanent collection and devoted it to the works of significant contemporary artists who have helped shape the world's current art scene. Through group and solo exhibitions, the museum displays works by a wide range of international painters, photographers, and sculptors. Its hours are Tuesday through Sunday noon to 6pm (Thurs to 8pm).

Across Broadway on the second floor of no. 594 is the:

5. **American Primitive Gallery** (☎ 212/966-1530), which displays a range of works produced by self-taught artists. Often with strong, simple messages or a touch of whimsy, this art can be a refreshing antidote to the often

The Art of Gallery Hopping

Even to the initiated, the art world and its gallery scene can seem intimidating. But don't sweat it—treat gallery hopping like a visit to the candy store and give an easy-going once-over to everything on display, and then choose to savor the few that appeal to you the most.

Storefront galleries are the most visible, but the majority of galleries hide on the upper floors of nonde-script buildings, often half a dozen or more per address. Most galleries are open to the public, unless they're hanging a new show, from 10 or 11am to 5 or 6pm Tuesday to Saturday. Mid- or late July to early September is the worst time to try to explore the art scene because many galleries shut down around this time.

Galleries present their works in the form of 4- to 6-weeklong shows, either solo exhibitions of a single artist or a group show featuring the work of several artists. The lifeblood of galleries is selling a few of the pieces,

overthought and overwrought works by formally trained artists that populate other SoHo galleries.

Turn south down Broadway, passing back by Dean and Deluca and the likes of Sephora, Benetton, and Banana Republic, until you hit Spring Street. Turn left on Spring Street. You're now heading out of traditional SoHo into the remnants of Little Italy. This area, bounded by Lafayette and Elizabeth streets, is a hipper, newer, happening scene that is more sophisticated and much less "touristy" than SoHo. It has a European flavor, a few modest galleries, and lots of good small restaurants and bistros.

Take a Break At 80 Spring St. at the corner of Crosby, **Balthazar** (☎ **212/965-1414;** www. balthazarny.com) is a trendy spot that faithfully replicates a large Parisian bistro, with high pressed-tin ceilings, lazily turning fans, and animated conversation rising from closely pressed tables. The talk is as likely to cover the but they know that the lion's share of people who pop by are just perusing the art, so don't feel shy about sauntering in. Also, don't feel as though you have to spend a certain amount of time in every gallery; galleries are accustomed to people who literally just poke their heads in, take a quick glance around, and withdraw quickly. You might zip through 10 shows before you find one that appeals to you.

Although you should take this walking tour during the day, the best way to catch a glimpse into the living New York art world is to attend the evening opening of a new show, most of which are open to the public. The *Village Voice* newspaper, the "Weekend" section of Friday's *New York Times,* and *The New Yorker* and *New York* magazines all list upcoming openings, as well as current shows. For even more complete information, pick up a free copy of *The Gallery Guide* at just about any museum or gallery.

European Union and the New York art scene as the latest Wall Street trend or Madonna video (the pop diva herself has been known to chow down here). Hors d'oeuvres include a velvety warm goat cheese and caramelized onion tart, and spinach and arugula ravioli. The grilled brook trout or chicken paillard salad are equally mouthwatering, and with entrees ranging from roasted salmon to bouillabaisse (on Fri) to plain old hamburger with *pommes frites,* there's something for everyone. Main dishes run $9 to $32; save room for dessert at the next stop. Balthazar is open daily noon to 1:30am (Fri–Sat until 2:30am), with Saturday and Sunday brunch served 11:30am to 4pm. If you just want to grab a quick bite, stop next door in the almost comically overpriced, but quite good, *boulangerie* (bread shop).

Continue east on Spring Street to animated **Lafayette Street,** home to funky antiques shops (lots of '50s and '60s stuff), cafes, and pop art's first officially sanctioned

---

Kid-Friendly Experiences

- Savoring a treat at Eileen's Special Cheesecake (stop 6)
- Getting lost in The Enchanted Forest toy store (stop 11)
- Exploring the endless art supplies at Pearl Paint (stop 15)
- Taking in the *trompe-l'oeil* Richard Haas mural (stop 23).

---

outlet store, **Keith Haring's Pop Shop** (off this tour, a few blocks north at no. 292). If you look to your right, you'll see that Lafayette Street forks half a block down. Cross Lafayette Street here at Spring Street to walk down the east side of Lafayette so that you can take the left-hand branch of the fork, called Cleveland Place. Another half a block down at 17 Cleveland Place and the corner of Kenmare Street is the tiny:

6. **Eileen's Special Cheesecake** (☎ 212/966-5585; www.eileenscheesecake.com). Eileen Avezzano started making cheesecakes in her kitchen for neighbors in the early '70s; now she sends them all over the United States. Cupped in hand-molded graham cracker crusts, these little pies are held by many (clients have included Robert Redford, Peter Falk, and Frank Sinatra) to be the best cheesecakes in New York. Two dollars will get you a mini-cheesecake in any of about 19 variations, from plain to fruit-topped to chocolate-and-raspberry swirl.

Continue on the short block down Cleveland Place to Broome Street and turn right. At the corner of Broadway, on your right, you'll see the flank of the:

7. **Haughwout Building.** This cast-iron building was built in 1857 for E. V. Haughwout's china and glassware company, one-time supplier to the White House. It is a perfect example of how the cast-iron movement brought aesthetic sensibilities of past eras (in this case Renaissance Italy) together with the practicality, technical skill, and replication perfection of the industrial age. The architect

used a single element (a window arch) from Jacopo Sansavino's Renaissance Biblioteca on Venice's St. Mark's Square and based this entire cast-iron facade upon it, taking what was once merely a single part of a complex Renaissance structure and repeating it 92 times to make a new, industrial whole. This building was the first to use the steam-driven Otis safety elevator, a contraption that freed buildings from limiting their height to a comfortable walk-up and allowed skyscrapers to soar.

Turn right up Broadway to admire the front of the Haughwout Building as you head back north. As you near Spring Street, look across Broadway to see the bits of marble facade that remain from the:

8. **St. Nicholas Hotel** (nos. 521–23). With its velvet pile carpets, silk chair covers, and embroidered mosquito nettings, this luxury hotel from the 1850s cost more than $1 million to build, but it reaped even greater profits during the heyday of downtown high society. The Civil War heralded the end of its glory days (it even served time as the area's Union Army headquarters), and when the glitterati scene moved uptown in the 1870s, it had closed for good.

Swing left on Spring Street. At the corner of Mercer Street is:

9. **101 Spring St.,** an 1870 cast-iron masterpiece with huge windows that architecturally looked forward to the age of skyscrapers.

Turn right onto Mercer Street a few steps and look across the street at one of the oldest houses surviving in SoHo:

10. **105 Mercer St.** Built in 1831, this house was already doing brisk business as a brothel by 1832. In the mid–19th century, SoHo was New York's largest, and most genteel, red-light district. Mercer Street was lined with houses of illicit pleasure, and a full two-thirds of Gotham's ladies of the night trolled the streets looking for likely clients and then plying their trade in rooms on the upper floors of buildings like this one. By the end of the Civil War, the cream of the prostitute crop had moved uptown (arm-in-arm with high society), and

SoHo's bordellos declined into houses of truly ill repute, fit only for drunken sailors.

Manhattan businesses began razing these old buildings to put up warehouses on the cheap property, and the cast-iron age was born. This brick house survived and is one of Manhattan's oldest former brothels still standing (it's now a private home).

Turn around to walk south down Mercer Street. In the next block on the right at no. 85 is:

11. **The Enchanted Forest** (☎ 212/925-6677; www.soho toys.com), a boutique hawking handmade and other innovative children's toys, books, and stuffed animals in a rain forest–meets–fairy tale setting.

Continue south to Broome Street. At the far corner, you'll see the:

12. **Gourmet Garage** (☎ 212/941-5850), a specialty foods and sandwich shop similar to Dean and Deluca, but oriented more toward organic, rather than imported, fine foods.

At the southwest corner of Mercer and Grand at no. 103 Grand St. is the chillingly expensive:

13. **Yohji Yamamoto** (☎ 212/966-9066), a Japanese designer clothing boutique with elegantly stylish wares. The fashion here is overwhelmingly basic black, but a Mondrian-print raincoat does make an occasional appearance on the racks.

Continue down Mercer to no. 31:

14. **Roland Feldman Fine Arts** (☎ 212/226-3232; www. feldmangallery.com). This gallery of the very avant-garde showcases the designs of some of the most interesting artists and architects working in America, such as Arakawa, Joseph Beuys, Leon Golub, Buckminster Fuller, and Andy Warhol.

Trek down the last stretch of Mercer to Canal Street, across which you'll see the unmistakable, dingy white-and-red edifice of:

15. **Pearl Paint** (☎ 212/431-793; www.pearlpaint.com) at 308 Canal St. Quite possibly the world's greatest art supply store, Pearl Paint (est. 1933) is certainly one of the

largest, offering more than 45,000 items on six floors, all at a discount. The mazelike tunnels of Pearl's narrow aisles are piled high with the raw materials of creativity, and are fun to explore even if you're not an artist (and irresistible if you are).

Cross back to the north side of busy Canal Street and walk 1 block west to turn right on:

16. **Greene Street,** which boasts the highest concentration of cast-iron facades in the world—50 buildings in these five SoHo blocks. The first block alone, between Canal and Grand, has the longest continuous row of cast-iron facades left anywhere, a full 13 of them lining the east side of the street (nos. 8–34). Across the street, no. 15–17 is a late example (1895) done in simple Corinthian style. Back on the right, no. 28–30 is known as the "Queen of Greene Street," perhaps the finest cast-iron building ever erected (and currently in dire need of a paint job). It was designed in 1872 by master Isaac F. Duckworth in an era when French tastes had superseded the original Italian leanings, as evidenced by the Second Empire–style facade with a mansard roof.

At Grand Street, detour right to see:

17. **91–93 Grand St.,** one of the most successfully illusory cast-iron facades. The frontage is made up of iron plates bolted together so seamlessly that the building appears to be made of cut stone blocks.

Turn right back up Greene Street, and immediately on your right on the third floor of no. 38 is:

18. **Artists Space** (☎ 212/226-3970; www.artistsspace. org), which curates exhibitions of young, undiscovered artists before they get embroiled in the capriciously trendy feeding frenzy of the gallery scene.

Across the street and a bit farther north (no. 49) is the:

19. **Jack Tilton Gallery** (☎ 212/941-1775; www.jack tiltongallery.com), showing contemporary painting and sculpture, both by individual artists (David Sher, Nancy Spero, Fred Tomaselli) and by theme ("New China," a collection of contemporary Chinese art, was one recent hit).

Continue north on Greene Street. As you cross Broome Street, look back over your left shoulder to see the elaborate:

20. **Gunther Building,** with its curved corner windows on the southwest corner of Broome and Greene streets.

A short way up the next block on your right (no. 72–76) rises the:

21. **"King of Greene Street,"** another cast-iron master-piece designed by that genius of the genre, Isaac Duckworth. The ornate and complex classical facade (which, hallelujah, was being cleaned as this edition went to press) makes liberal use of Corinthian columns and decorative detail.

Across the street at no. 79 is:

22. **agnes b. homme** (☎ 212/431-4339; www.agnesb.fr), SoHo's men's outlet for the famed French designer.

Continue north on Greene Street, across Spring Street, and past more high fashion newcomers like Ferragamo and Armani Casa. At Prince Street, cross to the right (east) side of the street, turn around, and look back across Greene Street to see the:

23. **Richard Haas mural.** If cast-iron facades were originally conceived of as illusory imitations of more expensive stone facades, then Richard Haas's *trompe-l'oeil* mural of a cast-iron facade is quite the bit of irony (ha!). Look for the contented cat sitting in a half-open "window" that helps complete the illusion.

Turn right to detour down Prince Street 1 block, past Ermenegildo Zenga, Miu Miu, and J. Crew to the corner of Mercer Street, where stands an old Manhattan holdover:

24. **Fanelli's Cafe** (☎ 212/226-9412). Established in 1847, this bar is the second oldest in New York, though it's carried the name "Fanelli's" only since 1922 (when it was a speakeasy). Within the turn-of-the-20th-century interior, a clientele of surprisingly regular-looking folk (not wacky artiste types) belly up to the bar or sit at the little tables noshing on bistro and cafe-type dishes. On my last visit,

the sea change in the neighborhood was succinctly summed up by graffiti on the men's room wall (always an interesting read here), a penned faux battle cry of "Gentrification NOW!"

After a refreshing mug of ale (and perhaps a bracing cup of soup from the sidewalk kiosk just around the corner on the Mercer St. side of Fanelli's), backtrack along Prince to Greene Street and turn right (north) onto it. At no. 136 on your right lies the:

25. **Phyllis Kind Gallery** (☎ 212/925-1200; www.phyllis kindgallery.com), which tends to show eccentric, sometimes self-taught, artists from across America— Chicagoans Roger Brown and Jim Nutt; Robert Colescott's historical, African-American-themed paintings; and photographer Alison Sarr.

    Helmut Lang has replaced the duo of important art galleries that were once at no. 142 (though you should slow down to see some of the impossibly gorgeous human beings walking in and out of this address: the famous Ford modeling agency is up on the third floor). At the end of the block on your right at no. 146–150 sits:

26. **Moss** (☎ 212/226-2190; mossonline.com), a housewares design store of exquisite taste, representing the best and most expensive of 20th-century design. It's something between a museum and a shop, showcasing everything that's hot, from the rubber vases of Holland's Droog Design and flexible plastic bookshelves that undulate along the wall to inventive flatware and the collective output from Italy's Alessi firm, including colorful cat-faced bottle openers, Robert Graves's whimsical teakettles, and phallic butane lighters.

    Double back down Greene Street to Prince and turn right (there's the Richard Haas mural again). Pop into no. 113 on your right, a branch of:

27. **The Metropolitan Museum of Art Shop** (☎ 212/ 614-3000; www.metmuseum.org/store). Across the street sits SoHo's bronze Goddess of Overfertility.

    Keep heading west on Prince Street a few doors to no. 126:

28. **Harriet Love** (☎ 212/966-2280), one of the original artist-era SoHo shops. It sells vintage jewelry and vintage and reproduction clothes for women.

   Turn right up Wooster Street, most of whose top galleries became overpriced design boutiques at the turn of this century. Still surviving on your left, at no. 141, is one of the many branches of:

29. **The DIA Center for the Arts** (☎ 212/989-5566; www.diaart.org). Although ostensibly they occasionally change the exhibition at this art, lecture, and symposia center, Walter de Maria's "groundbreaking" work *The New York Earth Room* has filled the space with 250 cubic yards of dirt (22 in. deep) since 1977. It's open September to May, Wednesday to Sunday noon to 3pm and 3:30 to 6pm. (If you have the chance while in New York, by all means visit the Dia Center's headquarters in the heart of Chelsea's gallery scene at 548 West 22nd St.)

   Turn around to backtrack south on Wooster Street, crossing Prince Street. On your right at no. 119 is home to the well-known gallery of:

30. **Tony Shafrazi** (☎ 212/274-9300), which still carries a torch for the 1980s Pop Art movement and the East Village Artists. Recent shows have spotlighted Jean-Michel Basquiat, Keith Haring, Julian Schnabel, Donald Baechler, and Kenny Scharf, but the gallery also offers works by Dennis Hopper and Francis Bacon.

   Continue down Wooster Street to no. 112, the boutique of:

31. **Cynthia Rowley** (☎ 212/334-1144; www.cynthia rowley.com), a young designer of women's fashions. All along this block (at nos. 120, 110, and 100) multiple outlets for the funky little **c.i.t.e.** (☎ 212/431-7272; www. cite-design.com), an antiques shop of kitschy or just plain nostalgic 1950s-era furniture and housewares and modern variations thereon, are mushrooming up.

   You have a block of breathing space continuing south on Wooster—passing boutiques for Patagonia, Chanel, and Movado—until just before you reach Broome Street, where on the right, on the second floor of no. 59, is:

32. **Brooke Alexander Editions** (☎ **212/925-4338;** www.baeditions.com), one of the most important contemporary print galleries in New York. Along with the occasional installation, the American and European artists shown here tend to be well established: Andy Warhol, Joseph Albers, Georg Baselitz, Lucien Freud, Jasper Johns, Donald Judd, Sol Lewit, Robert Mangold, Robert Mapplethorpe, Bruce Nauman, Claes Oldenburg, and Robert Rauschenberg, among many others.

    Keep walking south on Wooster Street. In the next block, at no. 35, is:

33. **The Drawing Center** (☎ **212/219-2166;** www.drawing center.org), a prestigious not-for-profit outfit that since 1976 has been instrumental in getting emerging and underrepresented artists' work some SoHo exposure. There are usually three annual experimental shows of new artists and one (held Apr–July) of museum-quality historic drawings (the likes of Rembrandt, Guercino, and architects Gaudi and Inigo Jones). Across the street at no. 40, the Drawing Center has opened "**The Drawing Room,**" for even more experimental projects and installations.

    Keep walking south; just past Grand Street on the left (no. 22 Wooster) is the:

34. **American Fine Arts, Co.** (☎ **212/941-0401**), specializing in conceptual contemporary art. Every spring, it puts on a show of the "Art Club 2000," a group of artists (mainly photographers) formed at Cooper Union.

    Just beyond it, at no. 18, is **Deitch Projects** (☎ **212/343-7300**), showing truly avant-garde (read: often silly) art. Return up Wooster Street to Grand Street. From there, take a left. At West Broadway—SoHo's burgeoning restaurant row—take a right to walk up the east (closest) side.

    Take a Break   The Cupping Room Cafe (☎ **212/925-2898**) at 359 Broadway has an eclectic menu, eclectic atmosphere (with some intimate corners), and a good selection of wines by the glass. On the $14 to $22 side of the menu, recommendable entrees range from pork chops with apple chutney to grilled mahimahi with tomato coulis. The sandwich half of the menu is somewhat more reasonable, running around $7 to $12 for the likes of burgers and fries or black forest ham with Jarlsberg on pumpernickel. For dessert, the unique white hot chocolate goes well with any of the to-die-for fresh cakes and pastries, which are all made on the premises.

Continue north up West Broadway, a street where the rising rents brought on by such new tenants as Ralph Lauren, Tommy Hilfiger, Emporio Armani, and DKNY have forced out most of the funky little shops, noted galleries, and dusty old bookstores. Half a block past Broome Street at no. 375, you'll find:

35. **Anthropologie** (☎ 212/343-7070; www.anthropologie. com), a mix of clothing, home wares, and odd sundries that evokes a warehouse-sized version of a Banana Republic store, but with a vaguely Dr.-Livingstone-I-presume tone.

At no. 383 Broadway is **O.K. Harris** (☎ 212/431-3600; www.okharris.com), another of the surviving '70s galleries in SoHo, which showcases large quantities of American art in a variety of styles and from a range of artists. Some people are attracted to its multiple large showrooms and seemingly inexhaustible supply of works to suit any taste; others scorn it as a "supermarket of art."

Farther up West Broadway at no. 393 is a second SoHo DIA Center (www.diaart.org), this one showcasing:

36. **The Broken Kilometer,** another semipermanent installation by Walter de Maria. One kilometer's worth of solid brass cylinder segments (500 of them, weighing 18.75 tons in total) lie in five rows in the room here (working against the optical rules of perspective, the distance between each cylinder increases as they get farther away from you, so they *appear* to be physically equidistant). The companion piece, *The Vertical Kilometer,* is a single, 1,000-meter-long brass rod sticking straight up . . . but sunk almost entirely into the ground near Kassel, Germany. The same artist also did *The Lightning Field* out

in the remote New Mexico desert. This set of 400 steel poles sticking out of the ground is arranged to make a grid one kilometer by one mile in an area with an abnormally high frequency of lightning and so act as a group of lightning rods, causing the electricity to play about the grid. The electricity-free, chopped-up New York version is open mid-September to May, Wednesday to Sunday noon to 6pm.

Keep heading north on West Broadway. Halfway up the next block (no. 429) is the gallery of:

37. **Nancy Hoffman** (☎ 212/966-6676; www.nancy hoffmangallery.com), a real '70s gallery. Both in its style and its artists, it has managed to remain virtually unchanged since the day it opened and SoHo was just coming into its own as a gallery scene. Hoffman displays high quality contemporary artists such as Marc Calderon and Rafael Ferrer. Perhaps the last of its breed, Nancy Hoffman is not considered the cutting edge anymore, but it's still an excellent gallery.

Continue up West Broadway to Prince Street and detour left to no. 160, on the left, the:

38. **Vesuvio Bakery,** a real old-fashioned Italian bakery that's been in the Dapolito family since 1920. The green-edged plate windows, which are frequently featured in films and photographs, are usually stacked high with bread leaned straight up against them, with a few ring-shaped loafs perched on top for effect.

Turn around and walk back east on Prince Street, crossing West Broadway, to no. 141 Prince St., the:

39. **Louis K. Meisel Gallery** (☎ 212/677-1340; www. meiselgallery.com), a major exhibition space for photo-realists such as John Clem Clark, Chuck Close, Richard Estes, Mel Ramos, and Edward Runci.

You're now just four blocks from where we started and the N, R, W, Q stop at Broadway.

Greenwich Village Literary Tour

Start: Bleecker Street between La Guardia Place and Thompson Street.

Subway: Take the 6 to Bleecker Street, which lets you out at Bleecker and Lafayette streets. Walk west on Bleecker.

Finish: 14 West 10th St.

Time: Approximately 4 to 5 hours.

Best Time: If you plan to do the whole tour, start fairly early in the day (there's a breakfast break near the start).

The Village has always attracted rebels, radicals, and creative types, from earnest 18th-century revolutionary Thomas Paine, to early-20th-century radicals such as John Reed and Mabel Dodge, to the Stonewall rioters who gave birth to the gay liberation movement in 1969. A Village protest in 1817 saved the area's colorfully convoluted lanes and byways when the city imposed a geometric grid system on the rest of New York's streets. Much of Village life centers around Washington Square Park, the site of hippie rallies and counterculture demonstrations, and the former stomping ground of Henry James and Edith Wharton.

Many other American writers have at some time made their homes in the Village. As early as the 19th century, it was New York's literary hub and a hot spot for salons and other intellectual gatherings. Both the Metropolitan Museum of Art and the Whitney Museum of American Art came into being here, albeit some 60 years apart.

The 20th century saw Greenwich Village transformed from a bastion of old New York families to a bohemian enclave of struggling writers and artists. Though skyrocketing rents made the Village less accessible to aspiring artists after the late 1920s, it remained a mecca for creative people—so much so that almost every building is a literary landmark. Today, the high cost of housing here means that most modern Villagers are upwardly mobile professionals. There still are, however, plenty of resident throwbacks to the '60s, latter-day bohemians with multiple body piercings, earnest NYU students, gawking tourists, funky shops, and great cafes that keep this one of the liveliest neighborhoods in town. It also remains one of Manhattan's most downright picturesque neighborhoods.

Though the focus of this tour is the Village's literary history, I think you'll also enjoy strolling along its quaint, tree-shaded streets lined with Federal and Greek Revival buildings. This tour is a long one, and you may want to break it up into two visits.

● ● ● ● ● ● ● ● ● ● ● ● ● ● ●

Begin on Bleecker Street, named for a writer, Anthony Bleecker, whose friends included Washington Irving and William Cullen Bryant, at:

1. **145 Bleecker St.** James Fenimore Cooper, author of 32 novels, plus a dozen works of nonfiction, lived here in 1833. Though he is primarily remembered for romantic adventure stories about the American frontier, Cooper also wrote political commentary, naval history, sea stories,

Greenwich Village Literary Tour

1 145 Bleecker Street
2 Circle in the Square
  Theater
3 The Atrium
4 172 Bleecker Street
5 189 Bleecker Street
6 Minetta Tavern
7 130-132 MacDougal Street
8 85 West 3rd Street
9 The Provincetown Playhouse
10 137 MacDougal Street
11 Sixth Avenue and West 4th Street
12 33 Cornelia Street

13 11 Commerce Street
14 75 1/2 Bedford Street
15 The Cherry Lane Theatre
16 Chumley's
17 17 Grove Street
18 45 Grove Street
19 59 Grove Street
20 The Stonewall
21 The corner of Waverly Place
   & Christopher Street
22 Gay Street
23 139 Waverly Place
24 116 Waverly Place

0		0.1 mile	**Ⓜ** Subway
0	100 meters		**☕** Take a Break

Fifth Ave.

34

33

32 **31** ☕

45 W. 10th St.   **finish here**

46 ★

W. 9th St.

Village Square

W. 8th St.

☕

University Pl.

Fourth Ave.

Broadway

Wanamaker Pl.

Ⓜ

Ⓜ

Astor Pl.

MacDougal Alley

Washington Mews

30

27 **28** **29**

Washington Sq. N.

26

25

WASHINGTON SQUARE PARK

Greene St.

Mercer St.

Lafayette St.

W. 4th St.

E. 4th St.

10
9

8

7

Ln.

6

5

4 **3** **1**

2

W. 3rd St.

Great Jones St.

E. 2nd St.

MacDougal St.

Sullivan St.

Thompson St.

LaGuardia Pl.

Bleecker St.

Broadway

Ⓜ

☕

★ **start here**

W. Houston St.

Ⓜ

E. Houston St.

25 82 Washington Place	**36** 138 West 13th Street
26 Washington Square Park	**37** 152 West 13th Street
27 19 Washington Square	**38** 91 Greenwich Avenue
North (Waverly Place)	**39** 1 Bank Street
28 7 Washington Square North	**40** 45 Greenwich Avenue
29 3 Washington Square North	**41** 139 West 10th Street
30 Washington Mews	**42** Patchin Place
31 25 East 11th Street	**43** Jefferson Market Library
32 21 East 11th Street	**44** 50 West 10th Street
33 The Salmagundi Club	**45** 37 West 10th Street
34 The Forbes Magazine Building	**46** 14 West 10th Street
35 The New School for	
Social Research	

and a group of novels about the Middle Ages. His father—judge, congressman, and Federalist Party leader William Cooper—founded Cooperstown, New York, the author's childhood home. This town was the setting for the author's *Leatherstocking Tales,* the epic of frontiersman Natty Bumppo (written over a period of 19 years) that includes *The Pioneers, The Last of the Mohicans, The Prairie, The Pathfinder,* and *The Deerslayer.* The town is more famous today as the home of the Baseball Hall of Fame.

James F. Cooper entered Yale at age 13 (not an uncommon occurrence in the early 19th century), but he was expelled in his junior year for pranks such as putting a donkey in a professor's chair. At 17, his aborted college career was followed by a stint in the merchant marines and the navy. His first novel, *Precaution,* was published in 1820. It created no great stir in the literary world, but a second novel focusing on the American Revolution, *The Spy,* appeared a year later and enjoyed vast success, as did his later books.

Continue west (walk right) to:

2. **Circle in the Square Theater,** 159 Bleecker St. Founded by Ted Mann and Jose Quintero in 1951 at the site of an abandoned nightclub on Sheridan Square, the theater moved to Bleecker Street in 1959. It was one of the first arena, or "in-the-round," theaters in the United States. Tennessee Williams's *Summer and Smoke* (starring Geraldine Page), Eugene O'Neill's *The Iceman Cometh* (starring Jason Robards, Jr.), Thornton Wilder's *Plays for Bleecker Street,* Truman Capote's *The Grass Harp,* and Jean Genet's *The Balcony* all premiered here. Actors Colleen Dewhurst, Dustin Hoffman, James Earl Jones, Cicely Tyson, Jason Robards, George C. Scott, and Peter Falk honed their craft on the Circle in the Square stage. In the early 1950s, Sunday lectures and readings at the theater featured Gore Vidal, Dorothy Parker, Tennessee Williams, Arthur Miller, and many other illustrious authors.

Across the street is:

3. **The Atrium** (no. 160), a 19th-century beaux arts building by Ernest Flagg that is today a posh apartment building. Before becoming the sadly defunct Village Gate jazz

Kid-Friendly Experiences

- Visiting 130-132 MacDougal Street, if they've read *Little Women* (stop 7)
- Stopping by 11 Commerce Street, where Washington Irving wrote "The Legend of Sleepy Hollow" (stop 13)
- Watching the performers in Washington Square Park (stop 26)
- Discovering the eclectic collections The Forbes Magazine Building (stop 34)
- Having afternoon tea at Tea & Sympathy (see the "Take a Break" box on p. 90)
- Getting a look at 14 West 10th Street, the home of Mark Twain, author of *Tom Sawyer* and *Huckleberry Finn* (stop 46).

club in the late 1950s, this former flophouse was Theodore Dreiser's first New York residence (in 1895, he paid 25¢ a night for a cell-like room).

Farther west is:

4. **172 Bleecker St.,** where James Agee lived in a top-floor railroad flat from 1941 to 1951, after he completed *Let Us Now Praise Famous Men*. Though the book enjoyed great popularity in the 1960s, it was originally scathingly reviewed and went out of print in 1948 after selling a mere 1,025 copies. When it was published, Ralph Thompson of the *New York Times* called Agee "arrogant, mannered, precious, gross," and his book "the choicest recent example of how to write self-inspired, self-conscious, and self-indulgent prose." *Time* called it "the most distinguished failure of the season."

Rallying from critical buffets during his Bleecker Street tenancy, Agee created the screenplay for *The African Queen* and worked as a movie critic for both *Time* and *The Nation*. He had to move from this walk-up apartment after he suffered a heart attack.

Nearby, the quintessential Village corner of Bleecker and MacDougal is a good spot for a breakfast break.

Take a Break **Café Figaro** (☎ 212/677-1100) at 184–186 Bleecker St. is an old beat-generation haunt. In 1969, Village residents were disheartened to see the Figaro close and in its place arise an uninspired and sterile Blimpie's. In 1976, the present owner completely restored Figaro to its earlier appearance, replastering its walls once again with shellacked copies of the French newspaper *Le Figaro*. Stop in for pastries and coffee or an omelet and absorb the atmosphere, or sit at a sidewalk table to watch the Village parade by. It opens at 10:30am Monday to Friday and serves a full, fixed-price brunch Saturday and Sunday from 10am to 3pm. They now present Jazz music nightly at 8pm and, of all things, belly dancing on Sundays!

On the opposite corner is:

5. **189 Bleecker St.** For several decades, beginning in the late 1920s, the San Remo (today Carpo's Cafe), an Italian restaurant at the corner of Bleecker and MacDougal streets, was a writer's hangout frequented by James Baldwin, William Styron, Jack Kerouac, James Agee, Frank O'Hara, Gregory Corso, Dylan Thomas, William Burroughs, and Allen Ginsberg. John Clellon Holmes wrote about the San Remo in his 1952 novel, *Go,* one of the first published works of the beat generation.

Take a right and head north on MacDougal Street to the:

6. **Minetta Tavern,** 113 MacDougal St. at Minetta Lane (☎ 212/475-3850), which was a speakeasy called the Black Rabbit during Prohibition. The most unlikely event to take place here in those wild days was the founding of De Witt Wallace's very unbohemian *Reader's Digest* on the premises in 1923; the magazine was published in the basement here in its early days. Since 1937, the Minetta has been a simpatico Italian restaurant and meeting place for writers and other creative folk, including Ezra Pound, e.e. cummings, Louis Bromfield, and Ernest Hemingway.

The Minetta still evokes the old Village. Walls are covered with photographs of famous patrons and caricatures (about 20 of which artist Franz Kline scrawled in exchange for drinks and food), and the rustic pine-paneled back room is adorned with murals of local landmarks. Stop in for a drink or a meal. The Minetta is open daily from noon to midnight and serves traditional Italian fare.

Minetta Lane is named for the Minetta Brook that started on 23rd Street and flowed through here en route to the Hudson. The brook still runs underground.

A little farther up and across the street stands an 1852 house fronted by twin entrances and a wisteria-covered portico.

7. **130–132 MacDougal St.** belonged to Louisa May Alcott's uncle, and after the Civil War, Alcott lived and worked here. Historians believe it was here that she penned her best-known work, the autobiographical children's classic *Little Women* (Jo, Amy, Meg, and Beth were based on Alcott and her sisters Abbie, Anna, and Lizzie, respectively). Alcott grew up in Concord, Massachusetts, the daughter of transcendentalist Amos Bronson Alcott. Emerson was a close family friend, and Thoreau taught the young Louisa botany. During the Civil War, Alcott briefly served as a Union hospital nurse in Washington, D.C., until a case of typhoid fever nearly killed her. Mercury poisoning from the medication she was given left her in fragile health for the rest of her life. Alcott later published a book of letters documenting her time as a nurse under the title *Hospital Sketches.* Henry James called Alcott "The novelist of children . . . the Thackery, the Trollope, of the nursery and schoolroom." Die-hard chauvinist G. K. Chesterton found himself admitting in 1907 that "even from a masculine standpoint, the books are very good."

    Turn right onto West 3rd St. Walk 1 block, just beyond Sullivan Street, to:

8. **85 West 3rd St.,** where Edgar Allan Poe lived, on the third floor, in 1845 (last window on the right). He wrote "Facts in the Case of M. Valdemar" here, and "The Raven" was published during his tenancy. Today, it's part of the NYU Law School, and the current residents claim that Poe's rooms are haunted.

    Double back down 3rd Street to MacDougal Street and turn right. On your left is:

9. **The Provincetown Playhouse,** 133 MacDougal St. (☎ 212/477-5048), which was first established in 1915 on a wharf in Provincetown, Massachusetts. Founders George Cram "Jig" Cook and his wife, Susan Glaspell, began by producing their own plays. One day, however, an intense 27-year-old named Eugene O'Neill arrived in Provincetown with a trunkful of plays, a few of which he brought for Cook and Glaspell to read. They immediately recognized his genius and were inspired to create a theater dedicated to experimental drama. The theater later moved to this converted stable, where O'Neill managed it through 1927. Many of O'Neill's early plays premiered here: *Bound East for Cardiff, The Hairy Ape, The Long Voyage Home, The Emperor Jones,* and *All God's Chillun's Got Wings.* That last play was especially radical for its time because of its portrayal of a racially mixed couple; black star Paul Robeson kissed white actress Mary Blair (literary critic Edmund Wilson's wife) on stage, prompting general outrage and Ku Klux Klan threats. Nevertheless, the play ran for 5 months.

Other seminal figures in the theater's early days were Max Eastman, Djuna Barnes, Edna Ferber, and John Reed. Edna St. Vincent Millay, whose unlikely life plan was to support herself as a poet by earning her living as an actress, snagged both the lead in Fred Dell's *An Angel Intrudes* and Dell himself (their love affair inspired her poems "Weeds" and "Journal"). Millay's own work, *Aria da Capo,* was produced here in 1919. Another notable Provincetown Playhouse production was e.e. cummings's *him,* a play with 21 scenes and 105 characters.

Katharine Cornell, Tallulah Bankhead, Bette Davis (who made her stage debut here), and Eva Le Gallienne appeared on the Provincetown stage in its early years. The theater was a great success, and O'Neill's plays went on to Broadway. But instead of basking in their popularity, Cook and Glaspell disbanded the company and moved to Greece, convinced that acceptance by the establishment signaled their failure as revolutionary artists. Though the Provincetown Players gave their last performance on December 14, 1929, this theater, fully restored in 1997, now presents plays by and for young people, as well as community playhouse–produced O'Neill works.

Next door is:

10. **137 MacDougal St.** Jack London, Upton Sinclair, Vachel Lindsay, Louis Untermeyer, Max Eastman, Theodore Dreiser, Lincoln Steffens, and Sinclair Lewis hashed over life theories at the Liberal Club, "A Meeting Place for Those Interested in New Ideas," founded in 1913 on the second floor of the house that once stood here. Margaret Sanger lectured the club on birth control, an on-premises organization called Heterodoxy worked to promote feminist causes, and cubist art was displayed on the walls.

Downstairs were Polly's Restaurant (run by Polly Holladay and Hippolyte Havel) and the radical Washington Square Book Shop, from which Liberal Club members more often borrowed than bought. Holladay, a staunch anarchist, refused to join even the Liberal Club, which, however bohemian, was still an "organization." The apoplectic Havel, who was on the editorial board of *The Masses* (see stop 38), once shouted out at a meeting where fellow members were debating which literary contributions to accept: "Bourgeois pigs! Voting! Voting on poetry! Poetry is something from the soul! You can't vote on poetry!" When Floyd Dell pointed out to Havel that he had once made editorial selections for the radical magazine *Mother Earth,* Havel shot back, "Yes, but we didn't abide by the results!" Hugo Kalmar, a character in O'Neill's *The Iceman Cometh,* is purportedly based on Havel. In a previous incarnation, this building was the home of Nathaniel Currier (of Currier and Ives).

Turn left onto West 4th Street and continue to the corner of:

11. **Sixth Avenue and West 4th Street.** Eugene O'Neill, a heavy drinker, nightly frequented a bar called the Golden Swan (more familiarly known as the "Hell Hole" or "Bucket of Blood") where the small park now stands. The bar was patronized by prostitutes, gangsters, longshoremen, anarchists, politicians, artists, and writers. O'Neill later used the bar as a setting for his play *The Iceman Cometh,* a script that was 12 years in the writing. Eccentric owner Tom Wallace, on whom O'Neill

modeled saloon proprietor Harry Hope, kept a pig in the basement and seldom ventured off the premises.

Cross Sixth Avenue, angle up the continuation of West 4th Street, and make your first left onto Cornelia Street looking for:

12. **33 Cornelia St.** Throughout the 1940s, film critic/poet/novelist/screenwriter James Agee lived on Bleecker Street and worked in a studio at this address. Here he completed final revisions on *Let Us Now Praise Famous Men,* which portrayed the bleak lives of Alabama share-croppers. The book originated in 1936 as an article for Henry Luce's *Fortune* magazine, which rejected the piece as too long and too liberal—the book's first pages contain a paraphrase from Marx's *Communist Manifesto:* "Workers of the world, unite and fight. You have nothing to lose but your chains, and a world to win."

Though a Harvard grad from an upper-class back-ground, Agee was extremely sympathetic to the plight of the poor (he once took a hobo into his home); dubious, if not downright cynical, about the very nature of journal-ism; and ashamed of the intrusive nature of his mission. "It seems to me," he wrote, "obscene and thoroughly terrifying . . . to pry intimately into the lives of an unde-fended and appallingly damaged group of human beings, an ignorant and helpless rural family, for the purpose of parading the nakedness, disadvantage, and humiliation of these lives before another group of human beings in the name of . . . honest journalism."

Next door, at 31 Cornelia St., **Caffé Cino** once stood. The cafe opened in 1958 and served cappuccino in shav-ing mugs. In the early 1960s, owner Joe Cino encouraged aspiring playwrights, such as Lanford Wilson, Sam Shepard, and John Guare, to stage readings and perform-ances in his cramped storefront space. Experimentation in this tiny cafe gave birth to New York's off-Broadway the-ater scene. Plagued by money troubles, Cino committed suicide in 1967; Caffé Cino closed a year later.

Continue down Cornelia Street to Bleecker Street and turn right. Cross Seventh Avenue, jog a bit left, and angle back down Commerce Street. Near the corner stands:

13. **11 Commerce St.** Washington Irving wrote "The Legend of Sleepy Hollow" while living in this quaint three-story brick building. Born into a prosperous New York family, he penned biographies of naval heroes as an officer in the War of 1812. In 1819, under the name Geoffrey Crayon, he wrote *The Sketch Book,* which contained the stories "The Legend of Sleepy Hollow," "Westminster Abbey," and "Rip Van Winkle." Irving was one of the elite New Yorkers who served on the planning commission for Central Park and was ambassador to Spain from 1842 to 1846. He coined the phrase "the almighty dollar" and once observed that "A tart temper never mellows with age, and a sharp tongue is the only tool that grows keener with constant use."

    Continue walking west on Commerce and turn left at Bedford Street to find:

14. **75½ Bedford St.** The narrowest house in the Village (a mere 9½ ft. across), this unlikely three-story brick residence was built on the site of a former carriage alley in 1873. Pretty, redheaded, feminist poet Edna St. Vincent Millay, who arrived in the Village fresh from Vassar, lived here from 1923 (the year she won a Pulitzer Prize for her poetry) to 1925. Ever a favorite among Village intelligentsia, the vivacious Millay perhaps best expressed her youthful passion for life in the lines:

    > *My candle burns at both ends;*
    > *It will not last the night;*
    > *But ah, my foes, and oh, my friends—*
    > *It gives a lovely light!*

    Other famous occupants of the narrow house have included a young Cary Grant and John Barrymore.

    Return to Commerce Street and turn left, where:

15. **The Cherry Lane Theatre,** nestled in a bend at 38 Commerce St., was founded in 1924 by Edna St. Vincent Millay. Famed scenic designer Cleon Throckmorton transformed the Revolutionary-era building (originally a farm silo, later a brewery and a box factory) into a playhouse that presented works by Edward Albee, Samuel Beckett (*Waiting for Godot* and *Endgame* premiered here),

Eugene Ionesco, Jean Genet, and Harold Pinter. In 1951, Judith Malina and Julian Beck founded the ultra-experimental Living Theatre on its premises. Before rising to megafame, Barbra Streisand worked as a Cherry Lane usher.

Nearby, in Commerce Street's bend, is **no. 48, a Greek Revival house** fronted by a bona-fide working gas lamp and built in 1844 for malicious merchant maven A. T. Stewart.

Continue around Commerce Street's bend to Barrow Street, where you turn right, and then turn left back onto Bedford Street. A few doors up on the right is:

16. **Chumley's,** 86 Bedford St. (☎ 212/675-4449), which opened in 1926 in a former blacksmith's shop. During Prohibition, it was a speakeasy with a casino upstairs. Its convoluted entranceway with four steps up and four down (designed to slow police raiders), the lack of a sign outside, and a back door that opens on an alleyway are remnants of that era.

Original owner Lee Chumley was a radical labor sympathizer who held secret meetings of the IWW (Industrial Workers of the World) on the premises. Chumley's has long been a writer's bar. Its walls are lined with book jackets of works by famous patrons who, over the years, have included Edna St. Vincent Millay (she once lived upstairs), John Steinbeck, Eugene O' Neill, e.e. cummings, Edna Ferber, John Dos Passos, F. Scott Fitzgerald, Theodore Dreiser, William Faulkner, Gregory Corso, Norman Mailer, William Carlos Williams, Allen Ginsberg, Lionel Trilling, Harvey Fierstein, Calvin Trillin, and numerous others. Even the elusive J. D. Salinger hoisted a few at the bar here, and Simone de Beauvoir came by when she was in town.

With its working fireplaces (converted blacksmith forges), wood-plank flooring, amber lighting, and old, carved-up oak tables, Chumley's lacks nothing in the way of mellowed atmosphere. Think about returning for drinks or dinner. A blackboard menu features fresh pasta and grilled fish. Open nightly from 5pm to an arbitrary closing time, Chumley's also offers brunch on weekends from 11am to 4pm.

Continue up Bedford to Grove Street, named in the 19th century for its many gardens and groves, and make a right to:

17. **17 Grove St.** Parts of this picturesque wood-frame house date from the early 1800s. A friend of James Baldwin's lived here in the 1960s, and Baldwin frequently stayed at the house. Baldwin, whose fiery writings coincided with the inception of the civil rights movement, once said, "The most dangerous creation of any society is that man who has nothing to lose."

Farther along this street is:

18. **45 Grove St.** Originally a freestanding two-story building, this was, in the 19th century, one of the Village's most elegant mansions, surrounded by verdant lawns with greenhouses and stables. Built in 1830, it was refurbished with Italianate influences in 1870. In the movie *Reds,* which is based on the life of John Reed, 45 Grove was portrayed (inaccurately) as Eugene O'Neill's house.

Ohio-born poet Hart Crane rented a second-floor room at 45 Grove St. in 1923 and began writing his poetic portrait of America, *The Bridge* (Hart depicted the Brooklyn Bridge as a symbol of America's westward expansion). Crane was born in 1899 with "a toe in the 19th century." His parents' marriage was a miserably unhappy one, and his mother, an artistic beauty subject to depression, concentrated her aesthetic energies on her son, giving him music and dancing lessons, taking him to art galleries, and providing him with every kind of children's book and classic. Although constant traveling with his mother kept Crane from finishing school, he was a voracious reader and brilliantly self-educated. By the time he was 17, his poetry had been published in prestigious New York magazines, and Nobel Prize–winning Indian poet Rabindranath Tagore was so impressed that he arranged to meet Crane when visiting Cleveland.

In later years, frustrated by frequent rejection from magazines and other exigencies of his craft, Crane would occasionally toss his typewriter out the window. Often moody and despondent, he was chronically in debt, plagued by guilt over homosexual encounters on the nearby docks, and given to almost nightly alcoholic binges; fellow Villager e.e. cummings once found him passed out on a sidewalk, bundled him into a taxi, and had him driven home. In 1932, returning by ship from Mexico (where, on a Guggenheim fellowship, he had been attempting to write an epic poem about Montezuma), Crane made sexual advances to a crew member, was badly beaten up, and jumped into the waters to his death at the age of 33.

Continue up the street to:

19. **59 Grove St.** English-born American revolutionary/political theorist/writer Thomas Paine died here in 1809. Paine came to America (with the help of Benjamin Franklin) in 1774, and in 1776 he produced his famous pamphlet, *The Crisis,* which was critical in rallying support for American independence, and begins with the words: "These are the times that try men's souls." After fighting in the American Revolution, he returned to England to advocate the overthrow of the British monarchy. Indicted for treason, he escaped to Paris and became a French citizen. While imprisoned in Paris during the Reign of Terror, he wrote *The Age of Reason.* He returned to the United States in 1802, where he was vilified for his atheism. Benjamin Franklin once said to Paine, "Where liberty is, there is my country." To which Paine replied: "Where liberty is not, there is mine."

The downstairs space has always been a restaurant, which today is called **Marie's Crisis Cafe** (☎ 212/243-9323). Though the building Paine lived in burned down, some of the interior brickwork is original. Of note is a WPA-era mural behind the bar depicting the French and American Revolutions. Up a flight of stairs is another mural (a wood-relief carving) called *La Convention,* depicting Robespierre, Danton, and Thomas Paine. In the 1920s, you might have spotted anyone from Eugene O'Neill to Edward VIII of England here.

At Seventh Avenue, cross to the opposite side of the wide intersection, walk around to the left of the little park, and head half a block up Christopher Street, the hub of New York's gay community, to no. 53:

20. **The Stonewall.** The current bar in this spot shares a name with its more famous predecessor, the Stonewall Inn. This bar was the scene of the Stonewall riots of June 1969, when gay customers decided to resist the police during a routine raid. The event launched the lesbian and gay rights movement and is commemorated throughout the country every year with gay pride parades. In the tiny Sheridan Square Park you just skirted, several of George Segal's realist sculptures honor the gay community. By portraying same-sex couples enjoying the park just like anybody else would, these sculptures point to the ludicrousness of marginalizing gay members of the community.

    Continue up the block to:

21. **The Corner of Waverly Place and Christopher Street.** The wedge-shaped Georgian Northern Dispensary building dates from 1831. Edgar Allan Poe was treated for a head cold here in 1836, the year he came to New York with his 13-year-old bride, for whom he would later compose the pain-filled requiems "Ulalume" and "Annabel Lee":

    > *I was a child and she was a child,*
    > *In this kingdom by the sea;*
    > *But we loved with a love that was more than*
    > *love—*
    > *I and my Annabel Lee.*

    Keep walking up Christopher Street to take a right onto:

22. **Gay Street.** Famous residents of this tiny street (originally a stable alley) have included New York Mayor Jimmy Walker, who owned the 18th-century town house at no. 12. More recently, Frank Paris, creator of Howdy Doody, lived here.

    In the 1920s, Ruth McKenney lived in the basement of no. 14 with her sister Eileen, who later married Nathanael West. It was the setting for McKenney's zany *My Sister Eileen* stories, which were first published in the *New Yorker* and then collected into a book. They were then turned into a popular stage comedy that ran on Broadway from 1940 to 1942, followed by a Broadway musical version called *Wonderful Town* and two movie versions, one of them starring Rosalind Russell. The house dates from 1827.

Mary McCarthy, the *Partisan Review's* drama critic and author of *The Stones of Florence* and *The Group,* lived in a studio apartment at no. 18 in the 1940s. During Prohibition, the street held several speakeasies.

At the end of the short street, take a left onto Waverly Place and look for:

23. **139 Waverly Place.** Edna St. Vincent Millay lived here with her sister, Norma, in 1918. Radical playwright Floyd Dell, her lover, who found the apartment for her, commented: "She lived in that gay poverty which is traditional of the Village, and one may find vivid reminiscences of that life in her poetry." An interesting note: Edna St. Vincent Millay's middle name was derived from St. Vincent's Hospital, which had saved the life of her uncle.

Cross Sixth Avenue to check out:

24. **116 Waverly Place.** Dating from 1891, the building has hosted William Cullen Bryant, Horace Greeley, Margaret Fuller, poet Fitz-Greene Halleck, and Herman Melville. Here Poe read his latest poem, "The Raven," to assembled literati. Waverly Place, by the way, was named in 1833 for Sir Walter Scott's novel, *Waverley.*

Return to Sixth Avenue and turn left (south) down it. Take another left onto Washington Place to:

25. **82 Washington Place,** residence from 1908 to 1912 of Willa Cather, whose books celebrated pioneer life and the beauty of her native Nebraska landscape. Cather came to New York in 1906 at the age of 31 to work at the prestigious *McClure's* magazine and rose to managing editor before resigning to write full time. As her career advanced, and she found herself besieged with requests for lectures and interviews, Cather became almost reclusive and fiercely protective of her privacy. She complained,

*In this country, a writer has to hide and lie
and almost steal in order to get time to work
in—and peace of mind to work with . . . If
we lecture, we get a little more owlish and self-
satisfied all the time. We hate it at first, if we
are decently modest, but in the end we fall in
love with the sound of our own voice. There is
something insidious about it, destructive to
one's finer feelings . . . It's especially destructive
to writers, ever so much worse than alcohol, it
takes their edge off.*

Band leader John Philip Sousa owned the beautiful
1839 building next door (**no. 80**).

Washington Place ends at:

26. **Washington Square Park,** the hub of the Village.
This area was once a swamp frequented largely by duck
hunters. Minetta Brook meandered through it. In the
18th and early 19th centuries, it was a potter's field (more
than 10,000 people are buried under the park) and an
execution site (one of the makeshift gallows survives—a
towering English elm in the northwest corner of the
park). The park was dedicated in 1826, and elegant residential dwellings, some of which have survived NYU's
cannibalization of the neighborhood, went up around the
square. At this time, it was the citadel of the stifling patrician gentility so evocatively depicted in the novels of
Edith Wharton. She defined Washington Square society
as "a little set with its private catch-words, observances,
and amusements" indifferent to "anything outside its
charmed circle."

The white marble Memorial Arch (1892) at the Fifth
Avenue entrance, which replaced a wooden arch erected
in 1889 to commemorate the centenary of Washington's
inauguration, was designed by Stanford White. One night
in 1917, a group of Liberal Club pranksters climbed the
Washington Square Arch, fired cap guns, and proclaimed
the "independent republic of Greenwich Village," a
utopia dedicated to "socialism, sex, poetry, conversation,
dawn-greeting, anything—so long as it is taboo in the

Middle West." Today, Washington Square Park would probably surpass any of this group's most cherished anarchist fantasies and might even lead them to question the philosophy altogether.

Along the square's north edge stand many of the surviving old homes, including, just west of Fifth Avenue:

27. **19 Washington Square North** (Waverly Place). Henry James's grandmother, Elizabeth Walsh, lived at this now-defunct address. (The no. 19 that exists today is a different house, the numbering system having changed since James's day.) Young Henry spent much time at her house, which was the inspiration for his novel *Washington Square,* later made into the Olivia de Havilland movie *The Heiress.* In 1875, James moved to Europe where he became an expert on expatriatism and penned many novels about Americans living abroad.

Farther east is:

28. **7 Washington Square North,** where Edith Wharton, age 20, and her mother lived in 1882. A wealthy aristocrat, born Edith Jones, Wharton maintained a close friendship with Henry James and, like him, left New York's stultifying upper-class social scene for Europe (Paris) in 1910, where she wrote the Pulitzer Prize–winning *The Age of Innocence.* Both she and James were immensely popular in Europe and were deluged with invitations (James once admitted to accepting 107 dinner invitations in a single year). Wharton wrote almost a book a year her entire adult life, while also finding time to feed French and Belgian refugees during World War I and take charge of 600 Belgian orphans. For these efforts, she was awarded the Legion of Honor by the French government in 1915. No. 7 was also once the home of Alexander Hamilton.

Nearby is:

29. **3 Washington Square North** (today the NYU School of Social Work). Critic Edmund Wilson, managing editor of the *New Republic,* lived here from 1921 to 1923. Another resident, John Dos Passos, wrote *Manhattan Transfer* here. Dos Passos, a fiery New York radical in the 1920s, became disillusioned with Communism after

journeying to Spain with Hemingway during the Spanish Civil War. He was appalled that the Marxist-backed Republicans executed his friend Jose Robles, himself a Republican supporter. The incident, which caused a break between Dos Passos and Hemingway when the latter refused to challenge the integrity of the Republican cause, was the basis of Dos Passos's next novel, *Adventures of a Young Man* (1939). His books thereafter also demonstrated a marked shift to the right. In the 1940s, Dos Passos returned to his native Virginia.

Make a left at University Place and another immediate left into:

30. **Washington Mews.** This picturesque 19th-century cobblestoned street, lined with vine-covered, two-story buildings (converted stables and carriage houses constructed to serve posh Washington Square town houses), has had several famous residents, among them John Dos Passos, artist Edward Hopper (no. 14A), and writer Sherwood Anderson (no. 54). No. 54 dates from 1834.

Double back to University Place and turn left to head north to the southeast corner of 9th Street, where stands the first of two possible places to:

Take a Break The more expensive and formal of the choices is the **Knickerbocker Bar and Grill** (☎ 212/228-8490) at the southeast corner of 9th Street and University Place. This comfortable wood-paneled restaurant and jazz club attracts an interesting clientele, including writers (Jack Newfield, E. L. Doctorow, Erica Jong, Sidney Zion, Christopher Cerf) and actors (Richard Gere, F. Murray Abraham, Susan Sarandon, Tim Robbins). Harry Connick Jr. got his start playing piano at the Knickerbocker, and Charles Lindbergh signed the contract for his transatlantic flight at the bar here. The restaurant is open daily for lunch/brunch from 11:45am; an eclectic menu offers entrees ranging from pasta dishes to bangers and mash to Southwestern paella.

For smaller appetites, head 2 blocks up to a branch of **Dean and Deluca,** 75 University Place, at 11th Street (☎ 212/869-6890 or 212/473-1908). It offers superior light fare (pastries, croissants, ham and Brie sandwiches on baguette, pasta salads) in a pristinely charming setting, usually enhanced by recorded classical music. Be sure to look up at the gorgeous plasterwork ceiling. It's open Monday to Thursday 8am to 10pm, Friday and Saturday 8am to 11pm, and Sunday 9am to 8pm.

This address is also a stop on the tour. When Thomas Wolfe graduated from Harvard in 1923, he came to New York to teach at NYU and lived at the Hotel Albert (depicted as the Hotel Leopold in his novel *Of Time and the River*), which stood at this address. Today the Albert Apartments occupy the site.

From University Place, turn left onto 11th Street to:

31. **25 East 11th St.** The unhappy and sexually confused poet Hart Crane (whom you met at stop 18) lived here for a short time. His neighbor at:

32. **21 East 11th St.** was Mary Cadwaller Jones, who was married to Edith Wharton's brother. Her home was the setting of literary salons; Henry Adams, Theodore Roosevelt, Augustus Saint-Gaudens, and John Singer Sargent often came to lunch, and Henry James was a houseguest when he visited America from Europe. Jones's daughter, landscape architect Beatrix Farrand, grew up here before designing such renowned outdoor spaces as the White House's East Garden and the New York Botanical Gardens' Rose Garden.

Continue to Fifth Avenue, cross it, and turn right. On your right is:

33. **The Salmagundi Club,** 47 Fifth Ave., which began as an artist's club in 1871 and was originally located at 596 Broadway. The name comes from the *Salmagundi* papers, in which Washington Irving mocked his fellow New Yorkers and first used the term *Gotham* to describe the city. *Salmagundi,* which means "a stew of many ingredients," was thought an appropriate term to describe the club's diverse membership of painters, sculptors, writers, and musicians. The club moved to this mid-19th-century brownstone mansion in 1917. Theodore Dreiser lived at the Salmagundi in 1897, when it was located across the street where the First Presbyterian Church stands today. It

was at the Salmagundi that Dreiser probably wrote *Sister Carrie,* a work based on the experiences of his own sister, Emma.

Cross 12th Street. At the northwest corner is:

34. **The Forbes Magazine Building,** 60–62 Fifth Ave., with a museum (☎ 212/206-5548) housing exhibits from the varied collections of the late Malcolm Forbes, who was famous as a financier, magazine magnate, frequent Liz Taylor escort, and father of one-time presidential hopeful Steve Forbes. On display are hundreds of model ships; legions formed from a collection of more than 100,000 military miniatures; thousands of signed letters, papers, and other paraphernalia from almost every American president; a remarkable even dozen of Fabergé eggs and other objets d'art fashioned for the czars; an exhibit of the evolution of the game Monopoly (natch); and changing exhibits and art shows. Admission is free. The galleries are open Tuesday to Saturday 10am to 4pm.

Make a left on 12th Street and you'll see:

35. **The New School for Social Research,** 66 West 12th St., which was founded in 1919 as a forum for professors too liberal-minded for Columbia University's then stiflingly traditional attitude. In the 1930s, it became a "University in Exile" for intelligentsia fleeing Nazi Germany. Many great writers have taught or lectured in its classrooms over the decades: William Styron, Joseph Heller, Edward Albee, W. H. Auden, Robert Frost, Nadine Gordimer, Max Lerner, Maya Angelou, Joyce Carol Oates, Arthur Miller, I. B. Singer, Susan Sontag, and numerous others.

Turn right up Sixth Avenue and left onto 13th Street to:

36. **138 West 13th St.** Max Eastman and other radicals urged revolution in the pages of the *Liberator,* headquartered in this lovely building on a pleasant tree-lined street. The magazine published works by John Reed, Edna St. Vincent Millay, Ernest Hemingway, Elinor Wylie, e.e. cummings (who later became very right-wing and a passionate supporter of Sen. Joseph McCarthy's Communist

witch hunts), John Dos Passos, and William Carlos Williams. The *Liberator,* established in 1919, succeeded *The Masses,* an earlier Eastman publication (see stop 38).

Further west along the block is:

37. **152 West 13th St.** Offices for the *Dial,* a major avant-garde literary magazine of the 1920s, occupied this beautiful Greek Revival brick town house. The magazine dated from 1840 in Cambridge, Massachusetts, where transcendentalists Margaret Fuller and Ralph Waldo Emerson were its seminal editors. In the '20s, its aim was to offer "the best of European and American art, experimental and conventional." Contributors included Marianne Moore, Hart Crane, Conrad Aiken, Ezra Pound, Theodore Dreiser (who once wrote an article claiming that American literature had to be crude to be truly American), and artist Marc Chagall. T. S. Eliot, who once grumbled of the *Dial,* "there is far too much in it, and it is all second rate and exceedingly solemn," nevertheless published *The Waste Land* in its pages.

Continue west on 13th Street, and make a left on Seventh Avenue, a right on 12th Street, and then another right for some afternoon tea.

Take a Break When Londoner Nicky Perry moved to New York, she was disappointed to find no proper British teahouses where she could get a decent cup of tea, so she opened her own in 1990. **Tea and Sympathy** (☎ **212/807-8329**), at 108 Greenwich Ave., is straight out of the English countryside, a hole-in-the-wall crammed with a few tables (always crowded), a friendly British wait staff, and plenty of old-time charm in the form of Anglo paraphernalia plastered over the walls. Elbow room is at a minimum here, but it's worth the squeeze for a $14 full afternoon tea, which includes a tiered serving tray stuffed full of finger sandwiches with the crusts cut off (cucumber and mayo or egg salad), cakes, biscuits, scones, jam, and clotted cream, plus, of course, a pot of tea (go for the Typhoo). Cheaper, bona fide British dishes include shepherd's pie, bangers and mash, and Welsh rarebit. For dessert, try a treacle pudding or warm ginger cake. Tea and Sympathy is open daily from 11:30am to 10:30pm.

From Tea and Sympathy, turn left to walk back down Greenwich Avenue to the corner of 12th Street and:

38. **91 Greenwich Ave.** At the beginning of the 20th century, Max Eastman was editor of a radical left-wing literary magazine called *The Masses.* This magazine published, among others, John Reed, Carl Sandburg, Sherwood Anderson, Upton Sinclair, Edgar Lee Masters, e.e. cummings, and Louis Untermeyer. John Sloan, Stuart Davis, Picasso, and George Bellows provided art for its pages, which a newspaper columnist dismissed thusly:

> *They draw nude women for The Masses,*
> *Thick, fat, ungainly lasses—*
> *How does that help the working classes?*

Reed wrote the magazine's statement of purpose: "To everlastingly attack old systems, old morals, old prejudices." *The Masses* was suppressed by the Justice Department in 1918 because of its opposition to World War I (it called on Woodrow Wilson to repeal the draft and claimed that America's enemy was not Germany but "that 2% of the United States that owns 60% of all the wealth"). Reed, Eastman, political cartoonist Art Young, and writer/literary critic Floyd Dell were put on trial under the Espionage Act and charged with conspiracy to obstruct recruiting and prevent enlistment. Pacifist Edna St. Vincent Millay read poems to the accused to help pass the time while juries were out. The trials all ended in hung juries.

Continue another block down Greenwich Avenue; turn right on Bank Street and look for:

39. **1 Bank St.** In 1913, shortly after the publication of *O Pioneers!,* Willa Cather, at age 40, moved to a seven-room, second-floor apartment in a large brick house here. Here she lived with her companion, Edith Lewis, and wrote *My Antonia* (the third of a trilogy about immigrants in the United States), *Death Comes to the Archbishop,* and several other novels. In 1920, H. L. Mencken called

My Antonia "the best piece of fiction ever done by a woman in America . . . I know of no novel that makes the remote folk of the western farmlands more real than *My Antonia* makes them, and know of none that makes them seem better worth knowing."

When she became successful, Cather rented the apartment above hers and kept it empty to ensure perfect quiet. Her Friday afternoon at-homes here were frequented by D. H. Lawrence, among others. Unlike many Village writers of her day, Cather eschewed the radical scene and took little interest in politics.

From Bank Street, take a left onto Waverly Place, cross 11th Street to take another left on Perry Street, and make a final right back onto Greenwich Avenue to:

40. **45 Greenwich Ave.** In 1947, William Styron came to New York from North Carolina to work as a junior editor at McGraw-Hill. He moved here in 1951 after a stint in the marines and the success of his first novel, *Lie Down in Darkness*. Styron originally showed manuscript pages from that novel, begun at age 23, to Hiram Haydn, a Bobbs-Merrill editor whose writing class he was taking at the New School. Haydn told Styron he was too advanced for the class and took an option on the novel.

Continue down Greenwich Avenue to West 10th Street and detour right to:

41. **139 West 10th St.** Today an Italian restaurant, this was the site, for decades, of a popular Village bar called the Ninth Circle. But it was in 1954 at a former bar at this location that playwright Edward Albee saw graffiti on a mirror reading, "Who's afraid of Virginia Woolf?" and, years later, appropriated it. He recalled the incident in a *Paris Review* interview: "When I started to write the play, it cropped up in my mind again. And, of course, 'Who's afraid of Virginia Woolf' means . . . who's afraid of living life without false illusions."

Double back up West 10th Street, cross Greenwich Avenue, and walk a block where you will see the gated entry to:

42. **Patchin Place.** The gate closing off Patchin Place is never locked; feel free to pass through it. This tranquil,

tree-shaded cul-de-sac has sheltered many illustrious residents. From 1923 to 1962, e.e. cummings lived at no. 4, where visitors included T. S. Eliot, Ezra Pound, and Dylan Thomas. The highly acclaimed but little-known Djuna Barnes (literary critics have compared her to James Joyce) lived in a tiny one-room apartment at no. 5. Reclusive and eccentric, she almost never left the premises for 40 years, prompting cummings to occasionally shout from his window, "Are you still alive, Djuna?"

Among other works, Barnes wrote a memoir called *Life Is Painful, Nasty, & Short . . . In My Case It Has Only Been Nasty* (it certainly wasn't short; she lived to the age of 90); an experimental poetic novel called *Nightwood* (for which T. S. Eliot penned an introduction); and a collection of poetry called *The Book of Repulsive Women*. Three of her one-act plays were produced at the Provincetown Playhouse in 1919 and 1920.

Louise Bryant and John Reed maintained a residence at Patchin Place for several years until Reed's death in 1920. During this time, he wrote his eyewitness account of the Russian Revolution, *Ten Days That Shook the World*. To avoid interruptions from callers at Patchin Place, Reed rented a room atop a restaurant at 147 West 4th St. to do his writing. Theodore Dreiser and John Masefield were also Patchin Place residents, the former in 1895 when he was still an unknown journalist.

Turn left out of Patchin Place to cross Sixth Avenue. Continue down West 10th Street, but look to your right as you cross Sixth Avenue to see the:

43. **Jefferson Market Library** at 425 Sixth Ave., a former produce market. The turreted, red-brick-and-granite, Victorian-Gothic castle was built as a courthouse in 1877 and named for Thomas Jefferson. Topped by a lofty clock/bell tower (originally intended as a fire lookout), with traceried and stained-glass windows, gables, and steeply sloping roofs, the building was inspired by a Bavarian castle. In the 1880s, architects voted it one of the 10 most beautiful buildings in America.

Head east down 10th Street to:

44. **50 West 10th St.** After his great success with *Who's Afraid of Virginia Woolf?*, Edward Albee bought this late-19th-century converted carriage house in the early 1960s. It's a gem of a building, with highly polished wooden carriage doors. Albee wrote *Tiny Alice* and *A Delicate Balance* here, the latter being a Pulitzer Prize winner. In 1994, he won a second Pulitzer Prize for *Three Tall Women*.

    Now look for:

45. **37 West 10th St.** Sinclair Lewis, already a famous writer by the mid-1920s, lived in this early-19th-century house with his wife, journalist Dorothy Thompson, from 1928 to 1929. Lewis fell in love with the recently divorced Thompson at first sight in 1927 and immediately proposed to her. When asked to speak at a dinner party, he stood up and said, "Dorothy, will you marry me?" and resumed his seat. Lewis later followed her to Russia and all over Europe until she accepted his proposal. Unfortunately, the marriage didn't last.

    Your final stop is:

46. **14 West 10th St.** When Mark Twain came to New York at the turn of the 20th century (at the age of 65), he lived in this gorgeous 1855 mansion. An extremely successful writer (Twain's first book was a travel book, *The Innocents Abroad*), he entertained lavishly. Born Samuel Langhorne Clemens, Twain was once a riverboat captain, and he took his pseudonym from the singsong calls of the sounding men stationed at the prows of Mississippi paddle boats ("mark twain" meant the waters were a safe 2 fathoms deep). Twain was famous for his witticisms, including a quip on the art of quipping: "How lucky Adam was. He knew when he said a good thing, nobody had said it before."

The East Village

Start: The Strand Bookstore at the intersection of Broadway and 12th Street.

Subway: Take the 4, 5, 6, N, R, L to 14th Street/Union Square station; walk south on Broadway.

Finish: Astor Place subway kiosk.

Time: 3 to 5 hours.

Best Time: Weekdays after 9:30am, when the Strand has opened.

Worst Time: Weekends, when some places may be closed; however, even then there's plenty to see.

Like other New York City neighborhoods, the East Village has reinvented itself time and time again in the years since its inception as part of Dutch governor Peter Stuyvesant's farm. Its current incarnation is the funky fringe of the city's arts and nightlife scene. From about 1840, one immigrant enclave after another has filled the neighborhood's town houses and tenements, and all of these people have left their stamp, from the early Irish and German settlers to the still-extant mix of Jews, African Americans, Latin Americans, Japanese, Indians, Eastern Europeans (especially

Ukrainians), and Italians. In that melting pot boils an important ingredient: latter-day-bohemian middle-class nonconformists who still arrive here daily from all over the country. This diversity is the East Village's defining characteristic.

In the '60s and '70s, this neighborhood was the hub of hippiedom. The action then centered on St. Mark's Place between Second and Third avenues where activist Abbie Hoffman lived. Other major players included Allen Ginsberg, activist Jerry Rubin, Timothy Leary, cartoonist R. Crumb, Paul Krassner (editor of *The Realist*), Andy Warhol, concert promoter Bill Graham, and an assortment of Indian swamis, witches and warlocks, tarot card readers, Hell's Angels, Hare Krishnas, flower children, and political radicals. East Villagers of those decades ate macrobiotic diets, took yoga classes, and lived in $30-a-month railroad flats with bathtubs in the kitchen (barely renovated, these apartments now rent for over $2,000 a month). They thrilled to Janis Joplin and the Grateful Dead at the Fillmore East, danced at Warhol's Electric Circus, listened to jazz at the Five Spot, read the *East Village Other* and the *Bhagavad-Gita,* and took in three-for-a-dollar features at the St. Mark's Cinema.

In the 1980s, the East Village took a stab at becoming the next SoHo, complete with chic galleries and nightclubs, co-op conversions, and escalating rents. A declining economy toward the end of the decade rendered the nascent art scene stillborn, but trendy clubs and upscale restaurants are still thriving today—as are the high rents. Hippies have been replaced by spike-haired punks, anarchists, and crack dealers as well as youthful yuppie types who, oddly enough, are now the ones eating macrobiotic and taking yoga. Old-time residents still find it jarring to see the suit-and-tie set hoisting beers at the local bars. But gentrification notwithstanding, the East Village remains one of New York's most vital districts, a last holdout of bohemianism.

• • • • • • • • • • • • • • • • •

Begin your tour at the northeast corner of Broadway and 12th Street, where you will see a beehive of activity surrounding the:

The East Village

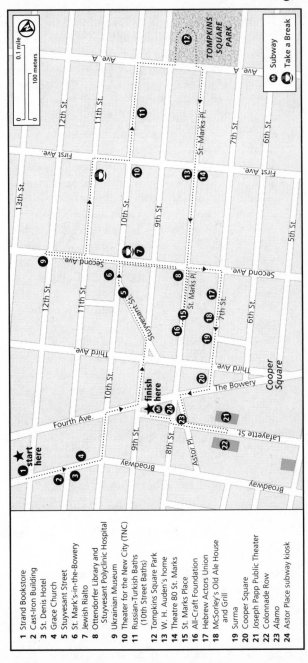

1 Strand Bookstore
2 Cast-Iron Building
3 St. Denis Hotel
4 Grace Church
5 Stuyvesant Street
6 St. Mark's-in-the-Bowery
7 Jewish Rialto
8 Ottendorfer Library and
  Stuyvesant Polyclinic Hospital
9 Ukrainian Museum
10 Theater for the New City (TNC)
11 Russian-Turkish Baths
  (10th Street Baths)
12 Tompkins Square Park
13 W. H. Auden's home
14 Theatre 80 St. Marks
15 St. Marks Place
16 All-Craft Foundation
17 Hebrew Actors Union
18 McSorley's Old Ale House
  and Grill
19 Surma
20 Cooper Square
21 Joseph Papp Public Theater
22 Colonnade Row
23 Alamo
24 Astor Place subway kiosk

M Subway
☕ Take a Break

0.1 mile
0   100 meters

1. **Strand Bookstore** (☎ 212/473-1452), which is the world's largest used bookstore and one of New York's most cherished institutions. The last survivor of Fourth Avenue's old Book Row, the Strand, named for the famous London street, was founded by Benjamin Bass in 1929. Currently run by his son, Fred Bass, and Fred's daughter Nancy, the Strand continues to be a favorite haunt of the city's rumpled intellectuals. Lee Strasberg, Anaïs Nin, and Andy Warhol were all regular customers during their lifetimes. Saul Bellow stops by when he's in town. The store has stayed open late so that Michael Jackson could peruse vintage children's books in privacy, and Sophia Loren once waited in a car outside while she sent actress Anna Strasberg in to pick up books for her. It's a bit of a madhouse at times, a maze of narrow aisles threading past towering stacks of books shelved haphazardly within their categories, but die-hard book lovers enjoy the treasure hunt.

   "Every book," says Bass, "eventually turns up here." The store boasts "8 miles of books." At any given time, its inventory comprises more than two million tomes, a variety of books on every subject you can imagine at bargain basement prices, including remainders, reviewer copies (sold at half price), used paperbacks, great art books, and hard-to-find novels. On the third floor is a huge collection of rare books where you might run across a second folio Shakespeare for $50,000, a first edition of *Uncle Tom's Cabin* for $2,500, or *The Story of the Exodus* with original Marc Chagall lithographs for $35,000. You can also find signed first editions (some for as little as $15). The Strand is open 9:30am to 10:30pm Monday to Saturday, 11am to 10:30pm Sundays.

   Walk downtown on Broadway to 11th Street. On the northwest corner is the:

2. **Cast-Iron Building.** Cast-iron architecture was in vogue in New York throughout the latter half of the 19th century, providing an economical means of embellishing buildings with ornate, often neoclassical facades. This one, constructed in 1868 to house the James McCreery Dry Goods Store, is one of the few buildings left standing

Kid-Friendly Experiences

- Exploring the Ukrainian Museum and purchasing an egg-decorating kit there (stop 9)
- Munching a cannoli at Veniero's Pasticceria (see the "Take a Break" box on p. 106)
- Playing on the playground and in the pool at Tompkins Square Park (stop 12)
- Spinning the *Alamo* sculpture and checking out the action on St. Mark's Place nearby (stop 23)

from the stretch of Broadway between 23rd and 8th streets that became known after the Civil War as "Ladies' Mile."

Luxury hotels and elegant department stores such as Wanamaker's, B. Altman, and Lord and Taylor opened up in this area; by the 1870s and 1880s, the high society of New York's Gilded Age enjoyed a splendor unrivaled in the New World. As writer Robert Macoy boasted in 1876, Broadway was "the grand promenade and swarm[ed] with the beauty, fashion, and wealth of New York. No avenue or street in London or Paris or Berlin, or any of our cities, can be compared with it." Toward the end of the 19th century, New York's wealthy families moved uptown, creating fashionable neighborhoods along Park, Madison, and Fifth avenues, and Ladies' Mile went into decline.

When McCreery's moved uptown in 1913, the Cast-Iron Building was converted first to office and warehouse space and then in 1971 to apartments. McCreery, an Irish immigrant who became a major New York merchandiser, was a patron of the arts, leaving much of his fortune to the Metropolitan Museum.

Across 11th Street on the southwest corner of the intersection is the building that used to house the:

3. **St. Denis Hotel.** Opened in 1848, the St. Denis represented the pinnacle of luxury and fashion to visitors for 60 years. Famous guests included everyone from Abraham

Lincoln to eminent Parisian actress Sarah Bernhardt. In 1877, Alexander Graham Bell demonstrated his recently patented telephone to New York notables here (he called someone in Brooklyn). All of the ornamentation that once graced the exterior was removed in 1917 when the St. Denis was converted to office space. If you walk around the corner on 11th Street, you can see some of the surviving facade on both of these buildings from another angle.

Continue downtown on Broadway; immediately on your left is:

4. **Grace Church.** One of the finest examples of Gothic Revival architecture in the United States, Grace Church was built between 1843 and 1847. It was the first masterpiece of 23-year-old architect James Renwick Jr., who would go on to design St. Patrick's Cathedral and the Smithsonian "castle." Renwick was also a regular parishioner, and his bust graces the west corner of the north transept. The garden in front of the parish house and rectory on Broadway was created by Calvert Vaux, who helped design Central Park.

In the middle of the 19th century, this was the most fashionable church in New York, with reserved pew seating costing $1,200 to $1,400. The church was always

Tom Thumb Ties the Knot

Despite its stunning architecture and traditional upper-class congregation, the most famous event ever to occur at Grace Church was a less than dignified one. P. T. Barnum arranged for the nuptials of two of his "biggest" sideshow stars, the diminutive Gen. Tom Thumb and his like-sized bride, Lavinia Warren, to be celebrated at the church. Though attended by the cream of society, their 1863 wedding exhibited all of the rowdiness and hoopla of a typical Barnum production. A parishioner who challenged sexton Isaac Hull Brown about the propriety of the affair received the response: "Even little people have the right to marry in a big church."

booked with weddings. Former New York City Mayor Philip Hone wrote in his diary that the stiff price of pews "may have a good effect; for many of them, though rich, know how to calculate, and if they do not go regularly to church, they will not get the worth of their money." He described the aisles of the church as filled with "gay parties of ladies in feathers and mousseline-de-laine dresses and dandies with moustaches and high-heeled boots."

In his opening sermon at Grace Church, Dr. Thomas House Taylor exclaimed, "I do not believe that the commonest laborer who has wrought on these stones can ever look back upon his work without a feeling of reverence and awe." The church is laden with stone carvings, the pulpit is of carved oak, and lofty columns rise from the handsome mosaic floors to support the vaulted ceiling. The building is constructed of hewn white marble, and its slender marble spire, atop a 110-foot tower, dramatically marks the horizon. Over the main entrance is a large, circular stained-glass window, and 45 additional interior Gothic windows sparkle with richly hued stained glass. Though all of the windows merit attention, note especially the five pre-Raphaelite windows by Henry Holiday: "Ruth and Naomi" and "Joseph and Benjamin" on the left aisle, "The Raising of Lazarus/The Raising of Jairus' Daughter" and "The Four Marys" on the right aisle.

The church is open 10am to 5:45pm on weekdays, Saturday noon to 4pm, and Sunday during services only from 8am. For information on church programs, Wednesday organ concerts, and services (they may begin offering tours after concerts and Sun masses), call ☎ 212/254-2000 or check out www.gracechurchnyc.org.

Turn left on 10th Street to follow the perimeter of the church grounds around to Fourth Avenue between 10th and 11th streets and see (on the west side of the street) the trio of houses built decades later in a Gothic Revival style faithful to the church itself. The northern house of the trio, the Grace Memorial House, was designed by James Renwick, Jr., himself; the others were designed by his firm.

Turn around to make your way south on Fourth Avenue. At 9th Street, you'll see the former Wanamaker

Department Store Annex looming over the southwest corner of Fourth Avenue and Wanamaker Place. Another Italianate cast-iron survivor from Ladies' Mile, the annex is now a Kmart.

Turn left to walk east on 9th Street, cross Third Avenue, and bear left onto the diagonal:

5. **Stuyvesant Street.** This street, one of the most charming in New York, is named for the dour Dutch peg-legged governor of Nieuw Amsterdam, Peter Stuyvesant, who built a large *bouwerie* (farm) for himself here in the mid-1600s. Stuyvesant Street was the entrance to his property, extending all the way to the East River. The governor's descendants continued to reside in the area into the 19th century. When city officials decided in 1811 to impose the street grid that characterizes Manhattan today, the wealthy families here saved the street from being razed; it is one of the few true east-west streets in the city.

The stately edifices along this street are most famous as wealthy private homes from the mid–19th century. However, the early 20th century saw many of them doing a brisk business as brothels (in particular nos. 25, 27, 29, and 31).

No. 21, a wide, Federal-style, three-story brick building known as the Stuyvesant-Fish House, was built in 1804 for the governor's great-great-granddaughter, Elizabeth, and her husband, Nicholas Fish, a Revolutionary War hero who had served at Valley Forge. Nicholas and Elizabeth's son Hamilton went on to become governor of New York, a U.S. senator, and secretary of state under President Grant.

Adjacent to the Stuyvesant-Fish House begins the Renwick Triangle, a group of 16 elegant brick-and-brownstone Anglo-Italianate town houses built in 1861 (nos. 23–35 on Stuyvesant St. and nos. 114–128 on 10th St.) and attributed to James Renwick. Architect Stanford White once lived at 118 East 10th St. You'll have to walk around the corner to see these 10th Street houses, but before you do, note the earliest house on Stuyvesant Street, no. 44, which was built in 1795 for Nicholas William Stuyvesant, a merchant. Its splayed lintels and Flemish bond brickwork are typical of the period, and the proportions of the doorway are an indication of this residence's original grandeur.

At the end of Stuyvesant Street, at 10th Street, is:

6. **St. Mark's-in-the-Bowery.** This late-Georgian Episcopal stone church, completed in 1799, replaced the 1660 chapel that was part of Peter Stuyvesant's farm. To the left and right of the Italianate cast-iron portico are statues of Native Americans by Solon Borglum called "Aspiration" and "Inspiration" (Borglum's more famous brother, Gutzon, carved the heads at Mount Rushmore) and busts of Peter Stuyvesant and Daniel Tompkins.

Tompkins (vice president under President Monroe and a former New York governor) is buried here in the cobblestoned courtyard, along with other prominent 18th- and 19th-century New Yorkers, including Mayor Philip Hone, several British colonial governors, Commodore Matthew Perry (who forced Japan to open diplomatic relations with the United States in the early 1850s), and Peter Stuyvesant himself—along with seven generations of his descendants. According to some accounts, there are more graves beyond the churchyard under Second Avenue.

St. Mark's Greek Revival steeple was added in 1828; its brick Parish Hall was designed by James Renwick in 1861, and its rectory was designed by noted architect Ernest Flagg in 1900. To get a look at the interior, you have to call ahead for an appointment (☎ 212/674-6377; www.stmarkschurch.org) or attend a service or cultural event here. After a 1978 fire, the top stained-glass windows had to be replaced; the new windows depict life on the Lower East Side. The original bottom windows (including one portraying Peter Stuyvesant) remain intact. If the garden courtyards are open, walk in and browse around. Especially lovely is the west courtyard behind the church, a tranquil oasis with benches shaded by ancient maple and London plane trees.

For many decades, St. Mark's Church has ardently supported the East Village arts community. Along with La Mama and Caffé Cino, it was a major birthplace of off-Broadway theater, nurturing playwrights such as Sam Shepard (whose first two plays, *Cowboys* and *Rock Garden*, were produced here). Another long-running church program is Danspace (www.danspaceproject.org), a venue for independent experimental choreographers; Isadora Duncan danced here in the 1920s, Martha Graham danced here in the 1930s, and more recently, Merce Cunningham performed here. The Poetry Project has featured readings by Kahlil Gibran, William Carlos Williams, Edna St. Vincent Millay, Carl Sandburg, Amy Lowell, Allen Ginsberg, and W. H. Auden (a member of the parish, Auden sometimes used to come to church in his bathrobe and slippers). St. Mark's was the setting for a wedding in the movie *The Group,* based on Mary McCarthy's bestseller.

Take a Break You have numerous choices here. Diagonally across the street from the church at 156 2nd Ave. is the famed **Second Avenue Deli** (☎ 212/ 677-0606), a New York institution for more than 40 years, serving up Jewish soul food nonpareil. Everyone patronizes this deli; you might see anyone from comic Jackie Mason to politico Geraldine Ferraro at the next table. Mafia don John Gotti was a regular before his imprisonment, even sending for takeout during his trial. Stop in for authentic pastrami and corned beef piled high on fresh-baked rye, plus chopped liver, *kasha varnishkes* (egg noodles stuffed with fried cracked wheat), knishes, and other deli favorites.

Or try the plain-Jane, inexpensive, and ultrafriendly **Ukrainian Restaurant,** 140 Second Ave. (on 9th St.), for Eastern European specialties such as blini, pierogi, potato pancakes, and borscht. The restaurant occupies the basement of the Ukrainian National Home. Incidentally, the Ukrainian National Home was the infamous Stuyvesant Casino in the early 20th century, the meeting ground for the Lower East Side's criminal element. Gangsters would throw parties here, forcing local merchants both to buy tickets and to pay for ads in a souvenir booklet. The ensuing fetes tended to be rowdy and were nicknamed after the "racket" they raised. The term "racket" would eventually be applied to all illegal gangster revenue-raising activities, and racketeering became the official crime they were committing.

Be sure to stop in front of the Second Avenue Deli, where brass-lined plaques set into the sidewalk (and the interior Molly Pecon Room) commemorate Second Avenue's heyday as the:

7. **Jewish Rialto.** New York's Jewish community increased in number and prosperity in the early years of the 20th century, and the new Jewish middle class turned Second Avenue between Houston and 14th streets into a center of Yiddish culture. Dubbed the Yiddish Broadway, it was the site of cafes, bookstores, and a score of Yiddish-language theaters, many of them lasting until the 1950s. Actors such as Jacob Adler (father of noted drama teacher Stella Adler) and comic actors Menashe Skulnik, Boris and Bessie Thomashevsky, and Maurice Schwartz took the stage every night in "immigrant-makes-good" plays, melodramas, and stock Yiddish comedy situations transposed to an American setting. Jacob Adler spearheaded a more serious dramatic movement, becoming famous for his "improved and enlarged" portrayal of King Lear and his proud version of Shylock. Thomashevsky adapted Shakespeare and Goethe to the Yiddish stage, and such well-known actors as Paul Muni, Edward G. Robinson, and Walter Matthau came up through the Yiddish theater.

Across from the Ukrainian Restaurant, at 135–37 Second Ave., are the:

8. **Ottendorfer Library and Stuyvesant Polyclinic Hospital.** These two ornately embellished redbrick facilities are the 1884 gift of Anna and Oswald Ottendorfer, publishers of a German-language daily newspaper called *Staats-Zeitung,* to the once-thriving German community of this neighborhood. Their aim was to nurture both the intellect and physical well-being of the immigrant population. The oldest extant branch of the New York City Public Library, the Ottendorfer's late Victorian building is adorned with terra-cotta wisdom symbols: globes, books, scrolls, owls, and torches. Its original name, the Freie Bibliothek und Lesehall, is still chiseled into the facade.

The adjacent clinic, even more elaborately adorned, features portrait busts of Hippocrates, Celsius, Galen, Humboldt, Lavoisier, and other scientists and physicians. The clinic was originally named the German Dispensary, but its administrators attempted to deflect anti-German sentiment during World War I by changing its name to the Stuyvesant Polyclinic Hospital. Architect William Schickel designed both buildings.

Walk north on Second Avenue past 12th Street, and look for no. 203 on your left. The fourth and fifth floors of this building house the:

9. **Ukrainian Museum** (☎ 212/228-0110; www.ukrainian museum.org). This small museum is committed to preserving the cultural heritage of the Ukrainian people. An assortment of folk art items are on permanent display, including traditional costumes and textiles of intricate embroidery and needlework. You'll find a large number of gorgeous, exquisitely decorated *pysanky,* decorated Easter eggs that, according to legend, will conquer evil if enough are painted. In ancient times, these eggs were created only by women and young girls—in secret, lest someone cast an evil spell by using fertilized eggs of chickens that had laid for the first time.

The museum also displays Ukrainian art, *rushnyky* (woven and embroidered ritual cloths traditionally used as talismans in births, weddings, funerals, and rites associated with the change of seasons), ceramics, and decorative brass and silver jewelry. The museum shop offers you the opportunity to buy examples of all of these items, as well as egg-decorating kits—pick some up for Easter (after all, the regular Paas decorating kit doesn't promise to help you conquer evil). Courses in Ukrainian folk crafts—embroidery, bead-stringing, making Christmas decorations—are also offered. The hours are Wednesday to Sunday 1 to 5pm. A small admission fee is charged.

Backtrack on Second Avenue to its intersection with 11th Street and turn left.

☕ **Take a Break** Eleventh Street between First and Second avenues is a small Little Italy, where an Italian community still flourishes. Stop in at the 1894 **Veniero's Pasticceria** (☎ 212/674-7070; www.venieros pastry.com) at no. 342; this Italian bakery and cafe is the perfect place for a cannoli and cappuccino. Veniero's is charming, with old-fashioned tile floors, beveled mirrors, an ornate pressed-copper ceiling punctuated by stained-glass skylights, and marble cafe tables. Its vast display cases offer myriad sweet temptations, including velvety cheesecake.

Note, too, some marvelous Italian food shops here, such as tiny **Russo's Mozzarella and Pasta Corp.,** 344 East 11th St., in business since 1908 as an emporium for imported and fresh cheeses and fresh pastas and sauce.

Walk downtown on First Avenue toward 10th Street. Just past the southwest corner of the intersection is the:

10. **Theater for the New City (TNC).** After a quarter of a century of presenting cutting-edge drama, poetry, music, dance, and visual arts, TNC's productions remain eclectic, politically engaged, fearless, multicultural, and creative. Go in and pick up a program or call the box office (☎ 212/254-1109; www.theaterforthenewcity.org) to find out what's on their current schedule.

Cross First Avenue and walk east (take a left) onto 10th Street. On your right, at no. 268, is a venerated New York institution, the:

11. **Russian and Turkish Baths, also known as the 10th Street Baths,** established in 1892 (☎ 212/674-9250). There were once numerous Turkish-style bathhouses in New York City; some of them, such as the Coney Island baths and the Luxor on 42nd Street, became the hangouts of gangsters and celebrities. In the 1970s, most New York baths became notorious yet again as (often raunchy) singles' scenes for gay men. With some bordering on orgy emporiums, most of these gay baths closed their doors in the mid-1980s when AIDS became widespread and widely feared.

The 10th Street Baths have remained staunchly straight and old-fashioned since their 19th-century inception. They are the last of the genre, open daily 11am (7:30am Sat–Sun) to 10pm, with an admission of $22 (more for various special massages and treatments; see box). They are co-ed except on Sunday from 7:30am to 2pm, which is reserved for men only, and Wednesday from 9am to 2pm, which is ladies' day.

The 10th Street Baths

The regular patrons of the 10th Street Baths, who come here for a *schvitz* (Yiddish for sweat), are quite a heterogeneous group. They include Orthodox Jews, Russian wrestlers, Wall Street brokers, rap stars such as L. L. Cool J, and, on co-ed days, fashion models. John F. Kennedy Jr. used to schvitz here, as did Frank Sinatra, Mikhail Baryshnikov, and Timothy Leary. In the early days of *Saturday Night Live,* Dan Aykroyd and John Belushi used to unwind with a postshow schvitz.

The setting is far from glamorous; the dank interior of the baths evoke a 19th-century dungeon. In the Russian Room, where 11 tons of rocks raise the temperature well above 200°F, patrons sit and steam, intermittently dumping buckets of ice water over their heads. Occasionally, they ask an attendant (in the old days, a deaf-mute incapable of following the conversations of mobsters) for a *platza,* a vigorous scrubbing with a brush made of oak leaves (it opens the pores and lets toxins sweat away). Afterward, the bathers flop into an ice-cold pool, wrap themselves in robes, and head upstairs for sustenance and conversation over a meal of borscht, schmaltz herring, whitefish salad, and kasha as well as fresh-squeezed juices. The premises also house massage rooms (offering everything from shiatsu to Dead Sea salt rubs), a small gym, tanning, a redwood sauna, cots to lounge on, and a pine-fenced sun deck on the second floor amid treetops.

One man who has visited the baths several times a week for 75 years summed up his loyalty to the place: "When I walk out from here, I am like a newborn baby . . . Why should I deny myself this little pleasure?"

Tenth Street next intersects with the first of the "Alphabet City" thoroughfares, Avenue A. Opening up from the southeast corner of the intersection is:

12. **Tompkins Square Park.** This beautiful 16-acre park was created on a salt marsh that was known as Stuyvesant

Swamp; the Stuyvesant family gave the land to the city in 1833. It is as much a focus of the East Village as Washington Square Park is of Greenwich Village. Like Washington Square, Tompkins Square was designed to be the hub of an upscale neighborhood, a vision that never materialized due to its out-of-the-way location. Although Washington Square attracts throngs of tourists, Tompkins Square remains a true neighborhood park. Many of its surrounding buildings date from the mid–19th century.

Head into the park at the 9th Street entrance. About halfway across the 9th Street walkway, through a brick portico, is an eroded monument commemorating a tragedy that was a swan song for the first immigrants to put their stamp on this area, the Germans. In 1904, the passenger ferry *General Slocum* burst into flame, was incinerated in under 15 minutes, and sank in the East River with over 1,200 aboard, most of whom were women and children from the East Village's "Dutchtown" ("Dutch" is a common corruption of *Deutsch,* which is German for "German"). The aging ship hadn't updated its safety equipment in years. The undrilled crew hefted the dried, old canvas fire hoses, but the useless things burst under the water pressure; frightened passengers grabbed rotted life preservers, which crumbled to dust in their hands. Many of the survivors, who lost friends and even entire families, found it emotionally impossible to continue living here after the disaster and moved to other German neighborhoods in the city. As Germans moved uptown, Eastern European Jews moved into the area.

Follow the park's walkways toward the southwest, and just behind the playground, you'll see the Temperance Fountain under a classical stone canopy, built in 1891 in hopes of convincing the thirsty to choose water over alcoholic spirits.

At the southwest corner of the park is a statue of 19th-century Congressman Samuel Cox, the "Postman's Friend," whose efforts to increase salaries and improve working conditions in the U.S. Postal Service made him a sort of patron saint of letter carriers.

Over the years, Tompkins Square has frequently been the site of riots and rebellions. In the 19th and early 20th centuries, it functioned as a venue for socialist and labor rallies. In 1874, one such gathering, resulting from a financial panic, was violently dispersed by city police, an event that became known as the Tompkins Square Massacre. Numerous peace rallies—not to mention some great rock concerts—took place here during the Vietnam War era.

Tensions in recent years, arising from the real estate industry's attempts to gentrify the neighborhood, have focused on the Christadora House (at the northeast corner of 9th St. and Avenue B), which was converted to high-priced condominiums by developers in 1987. It became the target of anti-gentrification forces when, in 1988, police attempted to enforce a curfew in Tompkins Square, and an ugly riot ensued. Officers clubbed and arrested not only protesters, but also innocent bystanders, and vandals did extensive damage to the Christadora. In the 1990s, the park was extensively renovated, and an encampment of homeless people was forced to move elsewhere, although they still make it their living room by day.

These tumultuous events notwithstanding, the park is essentially a recreational setting: Children entertain themselves in playgrounds, there's fierce hoop action on the basketball courts, swimmers cool off in the pool (open every summer), and people sunbathe on expanses of lawn and picnic under ancient elms.

Leave the park on the Avenue A side (west) and stroll west toward First Avenue along St. Marks Place (which, to the numerically minded, should be 8th St.), which is lined with neighborhood cafes, thrift shops, and tattoo parlors. Just across First Avenue on the north side of the street is:

13. **W. H. Auden's home,** at 77 St. Marks Place. Auden lived and worked in a third-floor apartment here, amid a clutter of books and manuscripts, from 1953 to 1972, a year before his death. Although he generally kept a low profile in the neighborhood, he occasionally breakfasted on scotch at the Holiday Cocktail Lounge next door (no. 75) and was a parishioner at St. Mark's-in-the-Bowery. Earlier in the century, the Russian Communist periodical *Novy Mir* was published at no. 77. Leon

Trotsky, a contributor, came by when he visited New York in 1917.

Across the street is:

14. **Theatre 80 St. Marks.** Until the advent of VCRs, revival cinema houses flourished in New York. This 160-seat facility was one of the last of the genre. It opened originally as a live theater in 1967; its first show, *You're a Good Man Charlie Brown,* played to sellout audiences for 4½ years. From 1971 on, proprietor Howard Otway, a former stage actor, dreamt up appealing double features and made his theater a shrine to the silver screen, adorned with photographs of the matinee idols of yesteryear. After Otway died in 1993, his son Lawrence decided to use the space for theatrical productions once more.

    Today, 80 St. Marks is the home of a classical repertory group called the **Pearl Theatre Company** (☎ **212/598-9802;** www.pearltheatre.org), which for 10 years was located in Chelsea. Unlike many contemporary theater companies, the Pearl does traditional interpretations of classic plays.

    Keep following this street west and you will soon reach the surreal center of the East Village counterculture:

15. **St. Marks Place,** between Second and Third avenues. Today populated by punks, anarchists, NYU students, and various street people who defy categorization, this hippie mecca of the 1960s and 1970s has declined to a state of general seediness. Adding insult to injury, it has been besmirched by a branch of the Gap, an advent as astonishing in the East Village as the appearance of McDonald's on Paris's Champs-Elysées. One landmark of days gone by is the Gem Spa, at the corner of Second Avenue, ever and always the area's most famous egg cream venue. Stop off for a glass of this New York–invented seltzer water, milk, and chocolate syrup beverage. Funky shops along the street that sell cheap jewelry, alt-rock T-shirts, leather, tapes, and CDs are augmented, unless there has recently been a bust, by peddlers hawking used books, incense, jewelry, and "tobacco" pipes.

    On the north side of the block, the bright blue building occupying nos. 19 through 25 is the:

16. **All-Craft Foundation,** an organization that helps homeless and drug-addicted people in the community. The building was once home to the Electric Circus, the disco that moved in after Andy Warhol's Exploding Plastic Inevitable (a multimedia event combining his films with live music, dancing, light show effects, and bizarre live action) at a bar called the Dom below. Before that, it was called Arlington Hall, a ballroom rented out mainly for neighborhood weddings, bar mitzvahs, and other celebrations.

A few gangster "rackets" were also held at Arlington, the most famous on January 9, 1914, when Italian mobster Jack Sirocco had the nerve to throw a ball here—in the middle of a Jewish gang-controlled neighborhood, and right in the midst of a turf war with neighborhood chief hood, Dopey Benny Fein. Fein was an "honorable thief" of sorts who controlled unions and played tough on the side of laborers against corrupt management. Sirocco, on the other hand, had his fingers deep in the capitalist pie. Just 2 months before the big "racket," Sirocco's outfit banged heads with Fein's gang, defending management's side in a strike, and one of Sirocco's goons offed a Fein flunky. As Sirocco's thugs climbed the stairs to the party here on January 9, Fein's boys, loitering in the doorways across the street, opened fire and plastered the Arlington's walls with a spray of bullets. Sirocco's men returned fire. Surprisingly abysmal shots on both sides, the gangsters collectively succeeded in hitting, and killing, only an innocent bystander. No one was ever convicted, but Fein's power was effectively broken. Several years later, Dopey Benny Fein quietly squealed to the district attorney, and then went straight.

Make your way back to Second Avenue and turn right, and then turn right again onto 7th Street. On the north side of the street, at no. 31, look for the granite facade into which is carved the name of the:

17. **Hebrew Actors Union.** During the heyday of Yiddish theater on Second Avenue, even the biggest stars used to pay regular visits to this building. Today, despite the almost total demise of the Jewish Rialto, the union is still active.

Farther along 7th Street is one of the few vestiges of the days when the East Village had a significant Irish population:

18. **McSorley's Old Ale House and Grill,** 15 East 7th St. (☎ 212/473-9148). One of New York's oldest watering holes, established in 1854, McSorley's looks (and smells) every bit its age. The wood floor is strewn with sawdust, and the pressed-tin walls are cluttered with a thicket of photos and newspaper clippings, all gone yellow with age and a century's worth of tobacco smoke, interspersed among an odd assortment of knickknacks and mementos.

    Over the years, luminaries from Peter Cooper to Brendan Behan have earned the right to a particular chair or bar stool, and the bar's beery charm was captured in Joseph Mitchell's *New Yorker* stories, later collected in a book, *McSorley's Wonderful Saloon*. Artist John Sloan immortalized the saloon's unique atmosphere in a painting called *A Mug of Ale at McSorley's* (1913). Perhaps the only significant change McSorley's has undergone in a century was to open its doors to women in 1971. If you drop in during an afternoon for a mug of sweet McSorley's ale (the food here, deli sandwiches and chili, is not notable), you'll catch a glimpse of the New York Peter Cooper knew.

    These days, 7th Street is the heart of a Ukrainian immigrant community some 20,000 strong. Representative of this community is:

19. **Surma** (www.surmastore.com), a store-cum-community center at no. 11, selling Ukrainian newspapers and books and Eastern European handicrafts. The latter include embroidered peasant blouses (Karen Allen wore one in the film *Raiders of the Lost Ark*), paintings, traditional porcelain, dolls, and *pysanky* (decorated eggs; see stop 9). Across the street is St. George's Ukrainian Catholic Church, its dome adorned with 16 beautiful stained-glass windows.

    Across Third Avenue from 7th Street is:

20. **Cooper Square.** Situated on this wedge-shaped lot are the chocolate-brown Cooper Union Foundation Building and a small park housing a bronze likeness of Peter

Cooper, who was an inventor, industrialist, philanthropist, and one of the great geniuses of his day. He made the bulk of his fortune through an ironworks and a glue factory, built the first steam locomotive in the United States (the Tom Thumb), developed the first rolled-steel railroad rails, and was instrumental in laying the first transatlantic telegraph cable. Cooper, a self-educated man from modest roots, believed that his wealth carried with it a responsibility to improve the working man's situation, so he founded the Cooper Union to provide free education in the practical trades and arts to any man or woman who wished to attend. A sense of Cooper as a benevolent, fatherly figure flows from the statue, and it's only natural: The sculptor, Augustus Saint-Gaudens, was able to attend Cooper Union's art school because of its founder's characteristic generosity.

The Cooper Union Foundation Building was completed in 1859. It was the first building in New York to use wrought-iron beams (another Cooper innovation), the forerunners of the steel I-beams that form the skeletons of present-day skyscrapers. The Italianate brownstone exterior remains much as it was in the 19th century. The interior, however, underwent extensive renovations in 1975.

From the lobby, you can see an elaborate and amusing carved-wood birthday card on the back wall, given to the founder by the senior class of 1871 to thank him for his 80th birthday gift of $150,000 to the school. To get past the security desk and down the stairs to the Great Hall, you must get permission from the Public Affairs office on the eighth floor of 30 Cooper Square. In keeping with Peter Cooper's designs for it, the Great Hall has functioned over the years as a free public forum in which great issues of the day are debated. Labor leader Samuel Gompers, free-love advocate Victoria Woodhull, and Sioux chief Red Cloud all spoke here, but perhaps the Great Hall's most famous moment occurred in 1860, when Abraham Lincoln's fiery "right makes might" antislavery speech carried public opinion in New York and sped him to the Republican Party's presidential nomination.

Also on Cooper Square are the offices of New York's most popular liberal rag and events magazine, *The Village Voice.*

Walk around Cooper Union, turn left on Astor Place, and then hang another left onto Lafayette Street. A few paces down on your left is the:

21. **Joseph Papp Public Theater** (☎ 212/260-2400 or 212/539-8734; www.publictheater.org). The Public, one of New York's most vital cultural institutions, is housed in the old Astor Library. This redbrick German Romanesque Revival–style palace, the first public library in the United States, was the lone public bequest of John Jacob Astor, who made millions in the fur trade and was a notoriously tightfisted landowner. In 1911, the library's collection was moved to the New York Public Library on 42nd Street. From 1920 to 1966, the Hebrew Immigrant Aid Society used the building to shelter and feed thousands of Jewish immigrants and help them gain a footing in the United States. When they moved out, city officials and Joseph Papp's New York Shakespeare Festival rescued the Astor Library from a developer who had planned to raze it to make way for an apartment complex. The building was designated a city landmark and became the permanent indoor home of the New York Shakespeare Festival.

The Public Theater opened in 1967 with the original production of *Hair,* which moved on to Broadway; in 1975, *A Chorus Line* followed suit, becoming one of the longest-running shows in Broadway history. Over the years, the New York Shakespeare Festival has utilized the Public's five stages to present new plays by such major playwrights as David Rabe, John Guare, David Mamet, Caryl Churchill, Sam Shepard, and Larry Kramer. Joseph Papp died in 1992, but the theater continues to thrive, with films, poetry readings, lectures, a cafe, a bookstore, and a late-night cabaret added to the offerings. Unsold theater tickets are often available as half-price "Quiktix" after 6pm (1pm for matinees Sat–Sun) in the lobby.

Across the street from the Public Theater is:

22. **Colonnade Row,** a group of row houses fronted by a crumbling marble colonnade. Of the nine row houses

built by developer Seth Geer in 1831, only four remain; the five on the south end were demolished to make room for the Wanamaker Department Store warehouse. Lafayette Street was once a quiet, posh residential district. John Jacob Astor lived here, as did members of the Vanderbilt and Delano families and writer Washington Irving. President John Tyler married Franklin Delano's daughter, Julia, here in 1844. The fashionable set moved uptown after the Civil War, and these houses have been in decline ever since.

Turn back and walk toward Astor Place. The black metal sculpture that dominates the traffic island in the middle of the intersection is the:

23. **Alamo,** known universally to area residents as "the Cube." Sculptor Tony Rosenthal built the piece in 1967 for a city-sponsored exhibition. He is reportedly pleased that the *Alamo* has become a participatory piece; it was built on a rotating post so that it could be positioned after installation, but it has become a tradition in the East Village for anyone feeling a bit rowdy to spin the Cube.

The next and last stop is on the adjoining traffic island across 8th Street and is the:

24. **Astor Place subway kiosk.** Earlier in the last century, almost every IRT subway stop in Manhattan had a kiosk much like this one. The Transit Authority inexplicably decided to tear them all down in 1911, but when the Astor Place subway station was restored in 1985, officials revived what had been a lost element of New York City's architectural scene. (Down in the station, Milton Glaser's mosaics and the ceramic low-relief tiles depicting beavers—the animal whose pelt made John Jacob Astor's fortune—are worth a look.) Peter Cooper would no doubt have been deeply satisfied to know that the archi-tect of the new kiosk was a Cooper Union graduate.

Midtown: The Concrete Jungle

Start: Grand Central Terminal.

Subway: Take the 4, 5, 6, 7, or the shuttle to 42nd Street/ Grand Central.

Finish: The Plaza Hotel.

Time: Approximately 4 hours, not counting time for browsing in shops and galleries.

Best Time: Weekdays, when Midtown is bustling but the attractions aren't as packed as they tend to be on weekends.

Worst Time: Rush hour (weekdays from 8:30–9:30am and 4:30–6pm).

If there's one area that defines New York in the popular imagination, it's Midtown. Concentrated here are dozens of the towering skyscrapers that are so closely identified with the city and its skyline. Lining Fifth Avenue and 57th Street are blue-chip art galleries, tony boutiques, chic department stores, and, increasingly, theme restaurants such as the Hard Rock Cafe that make New York the consumer capital of the world. Midtown is Manhattan at its most glamorous.

● ● ● ● ● ● ● ● ● ● ● ● ● ● ● ● ● ●

From the subway platform, follow the Metro North signs to the main concourse of:

1. **Grand Central Terminal.** Commodore Vanderbilt himself named the station "Grand Central" in the 1860s, despite the fact that it was out in the boondocks at that time. The present terminal was built in 1913. This engineering tour de force combines subways, surface streets, pedestrian malls, underground shopping concourses, and 48 pairs of railroad tracks into one smoothly functioning organism.

   Masterfully restored in 1997, the main concourse is breathtaking. It's one of America's most impressive interior spaces, with gleaming marble floors, sweeping staircases, and an aqua vaulted ceiling soaring 125 feet high. Twenty-five hundred pinpricks of electronic stars litter this "sky" with a view of a Mediterranean winter sky's constellations (seemingly backward, the zodiac symbols are supposedly represented as they would be seen from outside our solar system).

   When a developer announced plans to place a huge tower over the concourse in the 1970s, preservationists came to the rescue, with Jackie Onassis leading the charge. The terminal's design survived intact after a series of legal challenges that went all the way to the Supreme Court and resulted in a 1978 decision that upheld New York City's landmarks laws.

   Take a Break Grand Central has numerous spots where you can pick up coffee, a muffin, or a sandwich to fortify yourself for the tour, including a basement **Dining Concourse**—sort of like a mall food court, only with funkier choices.

   For something more substantial, head downstairs from the main concourse to the **Oyster Bar,** where passable seafood is served in a first-rate setting with a wide-vaulted ceiling Monday through Friday from 11:30am to 9:30pm.

Midtown: The Concrete Jungle

1 Grand Central Terminal
2 New York Public Library
3 Chrysler Building
4 The Algonquin Hotel
5 International Center of Photography
6 Gotham Book Mart
7 Rockefeller Center
8 Radio City Music Hall
9 West 52nd Street/21 Club
10 Berlin Wall
11 St. Patrick's Cathedral
12 New York Palace Hotel

13 The Waldorf-Astoria
14 St. Peter's Lutheran Church
15 Central Synagogue
16 Fuller Building
17 PaceWildenstein Gallery
18 Tiffany & Co.
19 Marlborough Gallery
20 George Adams
21 Mary Boone Gallery
22 F. A. O. Schwarz
23 The Plaza Hotel
24 Sony Wonder Tech Lab

Kid-Friendly Experiences

- Whispering in the "whispering gallery" at Grand Central Station (see the "Take a Break" box below)
- Skating at Rockefeller Center skating rink in winter (stop 7)
- Investigating F.A.O. Schwarz toy store (stop 22)
- Playing at Sony Wonder Tech Lab (stop 24)

You might take a seat at the counter for an appetizer of fried oysters, New Zealand greenlip mussels in Dijon dressing, or New England clam chowder. Full meals, including the catch of the day, are available in the dining room. The acoustics of the curved ceiling "whispering gallery" outside the restaurant's entrance allow people to stand in opposite corners and hold a whispered conversation.

Leave the main concourse via the 42nd Street exit and turn right. Walk west for 2 blocks and then make a left onto Fifth Avenue, where the:

2. **New York Public Library** (☎ 212/930-0830; www.nypl.org) sits in splendor, resembling a Greek temple with rows of Corinthian columns. Completed in 1911, this beaux arts palace, one of the greatest research libraries in the world, cost $10 million to construct, and President Taft himself attended the dedication ceremony. Everything inside was designed as a unit, from the marble walls to the chairs, stepladders, and wastebaskets.

Climb up the broad stone steps guarded by twin stone lions, named Patience and Fortitude by mayor Fiorello LaGuardia in the 1930s for the qualities he proclaimed New Yorkers would need to survive the Depression. Cafes on either side of the grounds, past fountains marked by classical statuary, offer umbrella-shaded tables. (Out back, Bryant Park is also littered with cast-iron tables. The park hosts a summer open-air film festival.)

The interior of the library contains manuscripts, maps, journals, prints, and more than 38 million volumes occupying 80 miles of bookshelves. You can sign up for tours (offered Mon–Sat at 11am and 2pm) at the information desk just inside the lobby, which is made entirely of unmortared Vermont marble. The staff can also point you to the library's current exhibits, its wonderful bookstore and gift shop, and the third-floor main reading room, a magnificent space extending the entire block-long length of the building. The library is open Monday, Wednesday, and Thursday 9am to 9pm, Tuesday 11am to 7pm, and Friday to Saturday 10am to 6pm (the shop is open Tues–Sun 11am–6pm).

Turn left out of the library to head uptown on the west side of Fifth Avenue. Look up and to your right as you cross 42nd Street to get a wonderful perspective view down the block to the:

3. **Chrysler Building.** At 1,046 feet, this Art Deco masterpiece reigned briefly in 1930 as the tallest building in the world until the Empire State Building came along. The stainless steel spire, with its hubcap ribs and thrusting gargoyles, creates one of the most beautiful and distinctive features of the Manhattan skyline.

Continue north on Fifth Avenue for 2 blocks to 44th Street, where you'll turn left. On the north side of 44th Street, at no. 27, is the Harvard Club, designed by McKim, Mead, and White in 1894 in an architectural style that mimicked Harvard's (at the time). The "Veritas" coat of arms tops the building. A few doors down at no. 37 is the Yacht Club, with a fanciful and flowing concrete facade of captain's cabin windows.

Continue along 44th Street. Near Sixth Avenue stands one of New York's most famous literary landmarks:

4. **The Algonquin Hotel.** Baltimorian H. L. Mencken began staying at the Algonquin on his frequent business trips to New York after he became the editor of *Smart Set* in 1914. Under Mencken's stewardship, the magazine published the early works of Eugene O'Neill, James Joyce, and F. Scott Fitzgerald. Nonetheless, Mencken

detested the city and remained unimpressed by its young bohemian writers ("The Village literati are scum," he once pronounced).

As *Smart Set* faded from influence in the 1920s, *Vanity Fair* began to take its place, counting Edna St. Vincent Millay, Elinor Wylie, and Theodore Dreiser among its contributors. In its offices at 19 West 44th St., Dorothy Parker, Robert Benchley, and Robert Sherwood served on the editorial staff. They began hanging out in the Algonquin, and soon their gatherings grew into the famous "Round Table," which also included Alexander Woollcott (drama critic for the *New York Times*), George S. Kaufman, Franklin Adams (columnist for the *New York World*), and Edna Ferber.

The group became famous for its witty, acerbic commentary on theater, literature, and the social scene, though Dorothy Parker herself played down its importance: "The Round Table was just a lot of people telling jokes and telling each other how good they were."

One of the regulars, Harold Ross, took it into his head to start a magazine that would incorporate the group's sophisticated, satirical outlook and rounded up investors to begin publication of *The New Yorker*, with offices set up nearby at 25 West 45th St. The first few issues were extremely uneven, but within a couple of years E. B. White and James Thurber had been added to the staff and were reshaping the magazine into one of the most prestigious publications in the country.

Even after the Round Table stopped gathering at the hotel, the Algonquin continued to count famous writers among its guests, including Gertude Stein and her companion Alice B. Toklas, F. Scott Fitzgerald, and William Faulkner, who wrote the acceptance speech for his 1949 Nobel Prize on Algonquin stationery.

To soak up this hotel's genteel ambience, consider having lunch or weekend brunch in the Rose Room. Or ensconce yourself with a cocktail in a comfortable sofa in the lobby lounge, where *New Yorker* writers frequently conduct interviews.

Across the street from the Algonquin, but light-years away in design, is the **Royalton Hotel.** Poke your head inside and take a look; the whimsically futuristic Jetsons-meets-fifties-lounge decor, created by Philippe Starck, has to be seen to be believed.

Cross Sixth Avenue (also known as Avenue of the Americas) and turn left. Before the corner of 43rd Street is the midtown branch of the:

5. **International Center of Photography** (☎ 212/857-0045; www.icp.org), massively renovated and expanded in 2000. ICP presents around 30 photography shows annually and is open Tuesday to Thursday 10am to 5pm, Friday 10am to 8pm, and Saturday to Sunday 10am to 6pm. Celebrating various trends, artists, and themes, these photo shows are some of the best in the city, well worth the admission price.

Double back north along Sixth Avenue to 47th Street, where you'll take a right. This block, between Fifth and Sixth avenues, is the **Diamond District,** where millions of dollars' worth of gems are traded every day. The business hustle on this block makes an unlikely setting for another literary sight, the:

6. **Gotham Book Mart** (☎ 212/719-4448), on the north side at no. 41. Originally founded in 1920 on West 45th Street, the store moved here in 1923. H. L. Mencken and his friend Theodore Dreiser once stopped in and, delighted to find some of their own works in stock, began to scribble dedications on many of the books, including the Bible, which they signed "With the compliments of the authors."

The store has hosted countless book publication parties, and the list of writers toasted here has included Dylan Thomas, Katherine Anne Porter, William Carlos Williams, W. H. Auden, Marianne Moore, Joyce Carol Oates, and Tennessee Williams. The most famous such gathering was the 1939 "wake" held to celebrate the publication of James Joyce's *Finnegans Wake.* In 1947, the store became headquarters of the James Joyce Society, whose first membership was purchased by T. S. Eliot.

Owner Frances Steloff (who died in 1989 at the age of 101) was known for lending a hand to perennially cash-strapped artists such as Henry Miller and John Dos Passos

(Martha Graham once borrowed $1,000 to stage her first dance performance).

Turn left up Fifth Avenue to 49th Street. On the right side of the avenue stands one of New York's most famous department stores, **Saks Fifth Avenue.** Immediately opposite Saks, head west into the promenade of:

7. **Rockefeller Center,** one of the most handsome urban complexes in New York. It encompasses 24 acres and 19 skyscrapers, extending from 47th to 52nd streets between Fifth and Sixth avenues. People scoffed at John D. Rockefeller in 1929 when he unveiled plans to build this "city within a city," because it was so far removed from what was then the commercial heart of New York. But Rockefeller proved all the critics wrong. His complex remade the map, drawing business uptown and setting the standard for future civic projects by incorporating public art and open spaces.

Stroll west through the **Channel Gardens** to Rockefeller Center's famous **skating rink.** In the summer, this area becomes an outdoor cafe; in cooler months, it's packed with skaters gliding along the ice to music and the twinkle of tiny lights in the trees. Each holiday season a giant Christmas tree stands here, towering over the promenade. Paul Manship's massive *Prometheus* lounges above the skating rink, beneath a quote from Aeschylus.

Take a look inside the lobby of **30 Rockefeller Plaza,** once the RCA Building and now renamed the GE Building. Above the black marble floors and walls are monumental sepia-toned murals by José Maria Sert. This Art Deco building was featured in the movie *Quiz Show.*

Just to the left of 30 Rockefeller Plaza, head west (right) on 49th Street to Sixth Avenue. You'll pass the wraparound corner windows with a digital news feed where early risers peer through the glass and wave in the hopes of becoming part of the backdrop during the filming of **NBC's *Today* show** just inside in the NBC News building.

When you reach Sixth Avenue, turn right and head uptown. A building boom in the 1960s and '70s transformed this area into a canyon of 50-story glass skyscrapers. Although the buildings aren't of great note individually, together they form an urban environment of considerable grandeur.

On the right side of Sixth Avenue, north of 50th Street, stands:

8. **Radio City Music Hall,** which was built in 1932 and has been restored to its original Art Deco elegance. Its original owner, Samuel "Roxy" Rothafel of Roxy Theater fame, ran it as a vaudeville house, but the enterprise was a flop, and Rothafel, in poor health, sold out to the Rockefellers. Eventually it became basically a glorified movie theater with Rockettes, but economic considerations and a 1979 overhaul returned it to live show business. Today, following an extensive 1999 restoration and pristinization, performances run the gamut from headliners like B. B. King or the Dixie Chicks, to shows like Comic Relief or Pokémon Live, to the annual Christmas Spectacular starring Radio City's own Rockettes and a nativity cast that includes live animals (picture camels and reindeer sauntering in through the Sixth Ave. entrance). Pricey hour-long guided tours (AAA and student discounts apply) take place every half-hour daily from 10am (11am Sun) to 5pm. Call ☎ **212/247-4777** for general information, or 212/307-7171 for tickets (Ticketmaster). You may buy tickets in the gift shop to the left of the entrance.

Continue up Sixth Avenue and take a right on:

9. **West 52nd Street,** designated "Swing Street" because this block holds a special place in jazz history. It was lined with a number of illicit speakeasies during Prohibition, and after its repeal, many of the establishments became jazz clubs, nurturing such great talents as Billie Holiday, Fats Waller, Dizzy Gillespie, Charlie Parker, and Sarah Vaughan.

The **21 Club,** below an iron balcony lined with lawn jockeys at 21 West 52nd St. (☎ **212/582-7200**), is still a popular restaurant and one of the few establishments to survive from this era. Operating as a speakeasy during Prohibition, it relied on several clever devices to guard against police raids, including a trap door on the bar that sent everyone's cocktails tumbling into the sewer when a button was pressed. Today it serves excellent food in a tavern atmosphere—if you can get a reservation in the popular dining room. The "smoking room" in front is open to anyone who wanders in and you can partake of a limited menu here. The club is closed weekends in summer and Sundays year-round.

Continue down 52nd Street. Near the end of the block, take a left through the modern passageway/lobby, numbered **666 Fifth Avenue,** which lets out on 53rd Street. In the tunnel, you'll pass by an undulating stainless steel wall waterfall designed by Isamu Noguchi.

When you pop out onto 53rd Street, turn right, cross Fifth Avenue and walk two-thirds of 53rd's next block to the second pocket-sized, granite-and-waterfall park, where sits a brief, graffiti-covered stretch of the:

10. **Berlin Wall.** Return to Fifth Avenue and take a left to cruise past glitzy outposts of high fashion, including Ferragamo, Cartier, and Versace. Between 51st and 50th streets rises the unmistakable neo-Gothic bulk of:

11. **St. Patrick's Cathedral,** the seat of the Archdiocese of New York and the largest Catholic cathedral in America. Designed by James Renwick in 1858 and modeled after Cologne's cathedral, this magnificent structure has twin spires rising 330 feet above street level. Construction took 21 years. Zelda and F. Scott Fitzgerald were married here in 1920.

Across the street as you exit, in front of 630 Fifth Ave., crouches Lee Lawrie's 1937 *Atlas,* one of New York's most famous statues, in 15 feet of bronze.

Walk along the north (left) side of the church on 51st Street. Cross Madison Avenue and take a right down it, admiring the Gothic-style tracery on the backside of St. Paddy's across the street. On your left, the block is filled with the brownstone-gone-amok mass of the:

12. **New York Palace Hotel,** also known as the Villard Houses after the Bavarian immigrant Henry Villard, who published the *New York Evening Post* and founded the Northern Pacific Railroad. He commissioned the unified buildings from McKim, Mead, and White in 1881. Today it's home to one of New York's most oft-reinvented and posh restaurants, **Le Cirque 2000 (☎ 212/303-7788;**

www.lecirque.com); the **Urban Center** (☎ 212/935-3592), whose bookshop is a treasure trove of tomes on architecture; and, through the central doors in the hotel itself, a compact architectural fantasyland of gilt, marble, sweeping staircases, crystal chandeliers, and opulent meeting rooms.

Take a left onto 50th Street and walk toward Park Avenue. As you look right down Park Avenue, you'll see the **Helmsley Building,** a lovely structure that sits astride the avenue, crowned with an elaborate cupola. The Helmsley Building is overshadowed by the **Met Life building,** one of New York's greatest architectural travesties (a big wedge of modernism at the end of one of New York's loveliest old-fashioned avenues).

Across Park Avenue, between 50th and 49th streets, stands one of the most famous hotels in the world:

13. **The Waldorf-Astoria.** For over a century, the Waldorf has been synonymous with wealth and luxury, though the hotel's present location only dates from the early 20th century. In 1897, in the midst of a devastating economic depression, society matron Mrs. Bradley Martin decided to hold a costume ball at the Waldorf (in the original building on Fifth Ave.) for 1,200 guests, who were to attend dressed in the style of the court of Versailles. When details of the preparations, rumored to top a quarter of a million dollars, hit the papers, outrage ran high. A huge squad of police officers, personally supervised by police commissioner (and future President) Teddy Roosevelt (whose wife was inside enjoying the festivities), had to be positioned around the hotel to prevent the great unwashed masses from venting their resentment.

Cole Porter and his wife lived for many years in one of the permanent apartments in the Waldorf Towers; one of the hotel's dining spots, Peacock Alley, still boasts his piano. Other famous residents have included Gen. Douglas MacArthur, Herbert Hoover, Henry and Clare Booth Luce, and the duke and duchess of Windsor. Gangster Lucky Luciano also lived here under an alias until he was forced to leave the Waldorf for less luxurious digs in the state penitentiary.

Between 50th and 51st streets on Park Avenue lies **St. Bartholomew's** (☎ **212/378-0200;** www.stbarts.org), a domed Episcopal church from 1918, which was begun in Romanesque style and switched to Byzantine halfway through construction. The church sports a three-arched main portal by Stanford White that came from the original St. Bart's once located down the street.

Take a Break St. Bart's may be the only church in New York with its own terrace cafe, **Café St. Bart's** (no phone). Under large umbrellas, with the Byzantine building shading you, you can dine alfresco on scrumptious fare, like the blue-crab burrito with chile oil, or the St. Bart's Classic—tomato-basil soup and a grilled farmhouse cheese sandwich. Main dishes run from $10 to $14. In summer, the terrace presents live music; in winter, the cafe moves indoors into an uninspired back room of the church's complex.

Walk around the left side of St. Bart's down 51st Street to Lexington Avenue and turn left up the east side of it. The **subway grating** on this block is perhaps the most famous in the world, ever since 1955 when one of its gusts of hot air sent the skirt of **Marilyn Monroe's dress** billowing right into pinup legend in *The Seven Year Itch.*

Continue north up Lexington to 53rd Street, where the corner office building (**no. 599 Lexington**) features Frank Stella's *Salto nel Mio Sacco,* a colorful 1985 work, in the lobby. Across 53rd Street from this building is the austere, glass-and-buffed-aluminum pinnacle of the Citicorp Center. This pillar of international finance incorporates, at the corner of 54th Street, the modern and angular:

14. **St. Peter's Lutheran Church,** built in 1977. This is a singularly hip house of worship. Adorned with sculpture by Louise Nevelson (check out the Erol Baeker Chapel of the Good Shepard), St. Peter's is famous for its Sunday evening Jazz Vespers, where many of the greatest names in jazz have performed. Besides the permanent Nevelson sculptures and a Pomodoro *Cross* out front, St. Peter's also regularly displays works by contemporary artists.

Just north of St. Peter's, at 55th Street and across Lexington, is the:

15. **Central Synagogue,** one of New York's finest examples of Moorish Revival–style architecture. The oldest synagogue in continuous use in the city, it was dedicated in 1870. It was recently renovated after a fire in 1998 left it scarred. The results of the renovation are breathtaking, reflecting the synagogue's original design, and adding new ornamental towers and crenellation on the outside, and over 5,000 vividly-colored wall stencils inside. Tours are available at 12:45 on Wednesday.

    Turn left on 55th Street and right on Park Avenue. On your left, you'll pass a **Mercedes showroom;** the curvilinear interior was designed by Frank Lloyd Wright long before he conceived of his more famous New York landmark, the Guggenheim.

    The longtime home to many of the city's top art galleries and upscale boutiques, 57th Street recently has been filling with theme restaurants and overblown chain retail stores. From Park Avenue, turn left along 57th Street, and you'll come to the beautiful black-and-white, Art Deco:

16. **Fuller Building** at the northeast corner of Madison Avenue and 57th Street. Look at the bronze doors, the marble fixtures, and mosaic floors and plan to spend some time browsing in the many art galleries housed here. Though a changeover from old guard galleries has occurred in recent years, the remaining galleries usually have one or two interesting shows each year. On the next block, you can browse the selection of caviar in the gourmet superstar store Fauchon.

    Across 57th Street at no. 32 is:

17. **PaceWildenstein Gallery** (☎ 212/421-3292), a major art gallery with specialty dealers spread out on several floors. The main gallery is devoted to 20th-century painting, drawing, and sculpture. It shows blue-chip artists such as Georg Baselitz, Alexander Calder, Chuck Close, Jim Dine, Jean Dubuffet, Agnes Martin, Louise Nevelson, Isamu Noguchi, Pablo Picasso, Mark Rothko, Julian Schnabel, and Richard Serra. On the 10th floor are **Pace Primitive Art** (African and Asian art) and **Pace Master Prints and Drawings** (prints and drawings by old masters such as Dürer, Goya, Matisse, Picasso, Piranesi,

Rembrandt, and Whistler). On the ninth floor is **Pace/MacGill** (20th-century photography) and on the third floor is **Pace Prints,** which carries contemporary prints by many of the same artists who show in the main gallery.

Continue along 57th Street to Fifth Avenue. On your left stretches the bejeweled:

18. **Tiffany & Co.,** with its windows full of amazing gems. (*Note:* Contrary to popular belief, it's not a good place to try and rustle up some breakfast, even if you are Audrey Hepburn.)

Cross Fifth Avenue and continue along West 57th Street. Halfway down the next block on your left at no. 40 (an office atrium entrance hallway down the right side of the passage) is the:

19. **Marlborough Gallery** (second floor; ☎ 212/541-4900; www.marlboroughgallery.com), one of the most reputable galleries in the world. Big stars here include the late Francis Bacon (Britain's de Kooning), Fernando Botero, Red Grooms, Richard Estes, Alex Katz, Antonio Lopez Garcia, Tom Otterness, Arnoldo Pomodoro, Larry Rivers, and Jacques Lipchitz.

Across the street, on the seventh floor of no. 41, is

20. **George Adams** (☎ 212/644-5665; www.artnet.com/gadams.html), which has been here for 30 years and features ceramicist Robert Arneson and other Bay Area artists, realists Jack Beal and Alfred Leslie, the colorfully eccentric paintings of Peter Saul, and Latin American painters such as Jose Bedia and Arnaldo Roche Rabell.

Return to Fifth Avenue, cross it again, and turn left (uptown) onto it, passing some of the city's most glamorous shops. On the east (right) side of the street, on the fourth floor of no. 745, you'll find:

21. **Mary Boone Gallery** (☎ 212/752-2929; www.maryboonegallery.com), a world-class gallery of contemporary art by Richard Artschwager, Ross Bleckner, Eric Fischl, Sean Scully, and Tim Rollins and K. O. S. (which stands for Kids of Survival). Rollins worked with street kids (K. O. S.) and, in an effort to control and engage them,

started them on art projects, sold to benefit the outreach program. The unlikely team became very influential in the 1980s art world. Also in this building is the McKee Gallery, which shows Philip Guston, a major abstract expressionist, as well as Jake Berthot, David Humphrey, Martin Puryear, and Jeanne Silverthrone.

Continue up Fifth Avenue. Just north of 58th Street is the toy store of every child's dreams and a New York institution since 1870:

22. **F.A.O. Schwarz** (☎ 212/644-9400; www.fao.com). You may remember Tom Hanks's famous dance interpretation of "Heart and Soul," performed here on a giant piano keyboard in the movie *Big*. The store is a wonderland of toys, with a menagerie of stuffed animals; fantastic, mobile Lego creations; squadrons of Barbie dolls; a candy shop; and command centers of video games where anybody can play.

Across from F.A.O. Schwarz stands the landmark:

23. **The Plaza Hotel,** built in 1907 and now part of the Canadian Fairmont chain. Back then, suites rented for $25 a night. Zelda Fitzgerald turned heads here by making a splash (literally) in the fountain in front of the hotel. The Fitzgeralds stayed here in September 1922 while looking for a home, and F. Scott used the Plaza as the backdrop for a crucial scene in his masterpiece, *The Great Gatsby*. Another famous guest, Frank Lloyd Wright, stayed in a suite overlooking the park while he designed the Guggenheim Museum. Young visitors will be familiar with the Plaza as the heroine's home in the children's classic *Eloise* (you can see her portrait, painted by *Eloise* illustrator Hilary Knight, across from the Palm Court); movie buffs will recognize the Plaza from *Crocodile Dundee, The Cotton Club, North by Northwest, Network, Arthur, Home Alone 2,* and, of course, *Plaza Suite*. Little-known trivia: 1920s Plaza chef Hector Boiardi decided to bottle his Italian pasta-and-sauce dishes for the masses; on the labels he phoneticized his name to Boy-ar-dee.

Head back downtown on Fifth Avenue. Detour left at 56th Street to the:

24. **Sony Wonder Tech Lab** (☎ 212/833-8100; www.sony
wondertechlab.com), a blatantly commercial, but undeni-
ably fun, high tech, hands-on "museum" of sorts for Sony
products. You can loop your own voice into famous
movie scenes on a mixing board, play with special effects
tricks on blue screens, and learn to operate robots. Oh,
and indulge in the free movie screenings and the coolest
setups for playing the latest PlayStation games. It's open
Tuesday to Saturday 10am to 6pm (to 8pm Thurs),
Sunday noon to 6pm.

Winding Down   There's no better place to stop for
an afternoon cocktail than the bar where the
Bloody Mary was invented: the **King Cole Bar in the
St. Regis Hotel,** 2 East 55th St. (☎ 212/753-4500),
adorned with a wonderful mural of the merry old
monarch himself. An elegant afternoon tea is served in the
Astor Court, a plush venue with a vaulted ceiling, trompe
l'oeil cloud murals, and 22-karat gold leaf on the delicate
stuccowork. Note that the management recently started
enforcing a "no sneakers" policy after 5pm in the bar.

The hotel itself is a landmark, built in 1904 by John
Jacob Astor. Ernest Hemingway, Alfred Hitchcock, and
Salvador Dalí all stayed at the St. Regis, and John Lennon
and Yoko Ono occupied suites here in the early 1970s.

Central Park

Start: Grand Army Plaza, at 59th Street and Fifth Avenue.

Subway: Take the N or R to Fifth Avenue.

Finish: The Vanderbilt Gate, which is the entrance to the Conservatory Garden, at 105th Street and Fifth Avenue.

Time: Approximately 5 hours, including lunch. If you want to explore the park more fully (stopping to visit the zoo for an hour or two, for instance), consider breaking this tour up into a 2-day-long excursion.

Best Time: Weekends, weather permitting, when the park hums with activity.

Landscape architects par excellence Frederick Law Olmsted and Calvert Vaux designed Central Park in the late 1850s, when the park's land was still on the outskirts of the city. Its creation ensured that New Yorkers would always have access to pastoral tranquillity. One of the world's most beautiful urban parks, Central Park is a recreational greenbelt of woodlands (26,000 trees), wisteria-shaded arbors, duck- and swan-filled lakes and lagoons, meadows, rambling lanes, gardens, fountains, pavilions, and picturesque bridges.

Central Park

W. 86th St. Ⓜ
W. 85th St.

85th St. Transverse

The Reservoir

map continues on next page

South Gate House

E. 85th St.
E. 84th St.

GREAT LAWN

Metropolitan Museum of Art

W. 81st St. Ⓜ

Delacorte Theater

16

Hayden Planetarium

15 14

Turtle Pond

E. 80th St.
E. 79th St.

American Museum of Natural History

79th St. Transverse

W. 77th St.

East Drive

Central Park West

Ramble

The Lake

13

12

11

W. 72nd St. Ⓜ

Strawberry Fields

72nd St. Transverse

E. 72nd St.

Fifth Ave.

Madison Ave.

10

Sheep Meadow

9

W. 66th St.
W. 65th St.

65th St. Transverse

8   6 7

E. 65th St.

3
2
1

West Drive

Central Drive

East Drive

5

Broadway

Hecksher Playground

The Pond

4

Columbus Circle Ⓜ

E. 60th St.

Central Park South

E. 59th St.
★ start here

0   0.1 mile
0   100 meters

W. 58th St.

1 Central Park Wildlife
   Conservation Center
2 The Arsenal
3 Delacorte Clock
4 The Pond
5 Wollman Rink
6 Chess and Checkers House
7 The Dairy
8 The Carousel
9 Sheep Meadow

10 The Mall
11 Bethesda Fountain
12 The Lake
13 Conservatory Water
14 Belvedere Castle
15 Shakespeare Garden
16 The Obelisk
     (Cleopatra's Needle)
17 Reservoir
18 Conservatory Garden

Encompassing 843 acres enclosed by stone walls, the park is 2½ miles long (extending from 59th–110th sts.) and a half mile wide (from Fifth Ave. to Central Park West), encompassing 6% of Manhattan's total acreage. It's the setting for numerous concerts, theatrical productions, and events ranging from marathons to bird-watching walks. There are playing fields for sports, bridle trails, 58 miles of walking and biking paths, boating lakes, a lovely zoo, gardens, playgrounds, and dozens of statues dotting the park; it even has its own website now: www.centralparknyc.org.

On weekends especially, musicians, acrobats, puppeteers, and other enterprising performers offer a wealth of free entertainment. The Central Park Conservancy and the NYC Parks Department have renovated more than a third of Central Park over the past decade, and the park today is safe, clean, and beautiful.

Consider starting out early (about 9am) with a leisurely breakfast at one of the plush luxury hotels near the entrance point: the Plaza's Palm Court or Edwardian Room, the Café Pierre at the Pierre, or the Fantino Restaurant at the Ritz-Carlton. All charge about $15, including tax and tip, for a continental breakfast and $25 for a full American breakfast. Much less pricey (but still very nice) is the Zoo Café, just inside the park, which offers terrace seating under a wisteria arbor; it's open, as is the zoo, from 10am on weekdays and from 10:30am on weekends and holidays.

An advance note on meals: Although Central Park offers a few restaurants, which I'll point out as we go along, they are a bit pricey. One cheaper alternative is noshing on street food from a hot dog stand, but I enjoy bringing along the makings of a picnic.

• • • • • • • • • • • • • • • •

Start at the southeastern corner of the park at Grand Army Plaza (see walking tour 10, stop 1). Cross 60th Street and take the wide, bench-lined path paralleling Fifth Avenue. Fork to the right through the brick gate and onto the path leading past the:

1. **Central Park Wildlife Center,** better known as **The Central Park Zoo** (☎ 212/861-6030; www.wcs.org). In spite of opposition by both Olmsted and Vaux, who

Kid-Friendly Experiences

- Paying a visit to the animals at the Central Park Wildlife Center (stop 1)
- Watching the Delacorte Clock performances (stop 3)
- Skating at Wollman Rink (stop 5)
- Riding on the Carousel (stop 8)
- Boating on The Lake (stop 12)
- Visiting the Alice in Wonderland statue group (stop 13)

feared losing natural scenery to gaudy attractions, some sort of zoo has been in the park since 1864. No other American city had a zoo in the mid–19th century, and the zoo's founders viewed the concept as a cultural coup for New York. Originally just a diverse collection of donated animals (Olmsted mockingly opined that they were mostly "pets of children who had died"), early zoo denizens included three African Cape buffaloes acquired by General Sherman during his Georgia siege, and circus animals quartered at the zoo in winter by P. T. Barnum. Eight monkeys (purchased rather than donated) were described in the *New York Times* in July 1871 as "comical 'Darwinian links'" (monkeys were of special interest in those early days of Darwinian theory). The zoo became a more formal establishment in 1934 when a quadrangle of redbrick animal houses was constructed.

In 1988, a renovated 5½-acre zoo opened its doors, replacing confining cages with natural-habitat enclosures and exhibiting a cross-section of international wildlife that comprises about 450 animals. Three major ecological areas are arranged around a formal English-style Central Garden that centers on a sea lion pool. The dense, jungle-like Tropic Zone, a rain forest environment with streams and waterfalls, houses an aviary of brightly hued birds, along with monkeys, alligators, reptiles, and amphibians. In the Temperate Territory, Japanese snow monkeys live on an island in a lake inhabited by Arctic whooper swans; this area also has an outdoor pavilion for viewing red pandas. The Polar Circle is home to penguins, polar bears, harbor seals, and Arctic foxes. If you do go in, make sure to visit the soothingly quiet Intelligence Garden, with wrought-iron chairs under a rustic wooden vine-covered pagoda. The zoo is open 365 days a year, 10am to 4:30pm. Admission is charged.

Across from the entrance to the zoo, up against Fifth Avenue, is:

2. **The Arsenal,** a fortresslike Gothic Revival building complete with octagonal turrets. Built in the late 1840s (predating the park), it housed troops during the Civil War and was the first home of the American Museum of Natural History from 1869 to 1877. Originally, its exterior brick was covered with stucco. Today, the brick is ivied, and the Arsenal houses park headquarters, zoo administration offices, and a third-floor art gallery. Walk around to the front entrance and note the stair railing made of rifles and the weapon-related embellishments on the facade. Inside, the 1935 WPA mural by Allen Saalburg merits a look if you're here on a weekday when the building is open. It depicts maps of New York parks, idyllic 19th-century Central Park scenes, and military themes.

Walk all the way around the Arsenal to continue up the zoo pathway, where you will see the:

3. **Delacorte Clock.** Atop an arched brick gate, this whimsical animated clock has been enchanting park visitors since the mid-1960s. Designed by Andrea Spadini, it features six dancing animals: a tambourine-playing bear, a kangaroo on horn, a hippo violinist, a Pan-like pipe-playing goat, a penguin drummer, and an elephant squeezing an accordion. On the hour and the half hour from 8am to 6pm, the entire animal assemblage rotates to nursery rhyme tunes, and two bronze monkeys atop the clock strike a bell. "Performances" on the hour are longer.

To get to the next stop, you'll have to double back past the Zoo Café and make the first right after exiting the gate, where a sign indicates the way to Wollman Rink. Bear left, cross and turn on to East Drive, and then veer left down the first sloped path you come to. Cross Gapstow Bridge over:

4. **The Pond,** originally the site of DeVoor's Mill Stream. On your left is a fenced-in bird refuge, the Hallett Nature Sanctuary. Make a right where the sanctuary fence ends and walk north around:

5. **Wollman Rink.** This popular skating rink, built into the northern bay of The Pond in 1951, provides skatable ice throughout the winter. The rest of the year it's drained and used for roller skating and in-line skating. The rink's refrigerating system broke down in 1980, and the ice rink remained out of operation until Donald Trump came to the rescue in 1986, bringing in his own construction specialists.

    Make the first right after the end of the rink, and then take the first left (an uphill slope) to the:

6. **Chess and Checkers House.** A gift from Bernard Baruch in 1952, this octagonal hilltop facility has 10 tables indoors and 24 outside for playing chess and checkers. The outdoor tables are under a rustic wooden arbor covered with vines. If you neglected to bring your own chess or checkers, you can borrow a set, just ahead on the path and to the right, at:

7. **The Dairy.** This Gothic Revival storybook stone cottage, designed by Vaux in 1870, originally served fresh milk and snacks to children. Cows were stabled in a nearby building. Today, the Dairy serves as a park information center, which is open Tuesday to Sunday 11am to 5pm, and houses exhibits on the design and history of the park. You can pick up an events calendar and informative brochures here and check out video information terminals.

    Double back, going around the right (west) side of the Chess and Checkers House. Duck through the tunnel (Playmates Arch) under Center Drive to:

8. **The Carousel.** This charming Victorian merry-go-round, which was originally turned by a blind mule and a horse, is one of the oldest concessions in the park. Its calliope has been playing old-fashioned tunes since 1872. The colorful whirling steeds are among the largest carousel horses in the world. Go ahead: Take the 90¢ ride.

    Continuing west (take the path left of the carousel), you'll be walking past the Heckscher ball fields. When you come to West Drive, turn right (north) and walk a short way. Tavern on the Green is across the street, behind the trees.

Take a Break **Tavern on the Green** is located in the park at West 67th Street (☎ 212/873-3200; www.tavernonthegreen.com). The original Victorian building was erected in 1870 to house the 200 sheep that grazed on the Sheep Meadow (see stop 9). The dazzling dining room, which Mayor Fiorello LaGuardia opened with a brass key, dates from 1934. In 1976, Hollywood mogul Werner LeRoy sank $20 million in renovating the Tavern as a setting for celebrity-studded parties, film premieres, and political functions. The food is nothing spectacular, but the sylvan setting makes for a memorable lunch atmosphere. It offers patio seating under the trees in a magnificent flower garden where 40,000 bulbs blossom year-round. The lavish, glass-enclosed Crystal Room offers indoor dining with verdant park views.

Make a right on the first path you come to after Tavern on the Green as you make your way north on West Drive. The path borders the:

9. **Sheep Meadow.** Originally mandated as a military parade ground, about which Olmsted was less than enthusiastic, Sheep Meadow took on a more peaceful incarnation in 1878. Until 1934, a flock of Southdown sheep grazed here, tended by a shepherd. Though undoubtedly picturesque, the sheep became deformed from inbreeding and were banished (though only to Prospect Park in Brooklyn) by parks commissioner Robert Moses; the shepherd was reassigned to the lion house in the zoo. During the 1960s, Sheep Meadow was a hippie haven and the setting for antiwar protests, love-ins, be-ins, and, after the 1969 Stonewall riots that launched the gay pride movement, a gay-in. Today the lush, green Sheep Meadow is a popular spot for kite flyers, sunbathers, and Frisbee players—a tranquil oasis where loud radios are off-limits.

Follow the fence on your right, and make a right where it turns onto the gravel path of Lilac Walk. After you pass the volleyball court area, cross the road and look for the bronze *Indian Hunter* statue (1869) by 19th-century American artist John Quincy Adams Ward. Straight ahead (look for a group of statues), turn left up:

10. **The Mall.** Designed as a Versailles-like grand promenade, this shaded formal walkway, about a quarter of a mile in length, is bordered by a double row of stately American elms that form a cathedral arch overhead. At its entrance are statues of Columbus (created in 1892 to mark the 400th anniversary of his voyage), Shakespeare (like the *Indian Hunter,* by J. Q. A. Ward; Shakespearean actor Edwin Booth laid its cornerstone), Robert Burns, Sir Walter Scott, and American poet Fitz-Greene Halleck.

   Make the first right at the end of the Mall and continue north around the back of the bandshell through the Wisteria Pergola. At the opposite end of the Mall, across East 72nd Street, a broad stairway—its massive sandstone balustrade ornately decorated with birds, flowers, and fruit—descends to one of the park's most stunning vistas:

11. **Bethesda Fountain.** Emma Stebbins's biblically inspired, neoclassical, winged Bethesda (the "angel of the waters") tops a vast, triple-tiered stone fountain with the lake forming a scenic backdrop. Its setting is Vaux's part-Gothic, part-Romanesque terrace, which is the heart of the park and one of its most popular venues. Like Sheep Meadow, Bethesda Fountain was a hippie hub in the 1960s, filled with counterculture types demonstrating against the Vietnam War, smoking pot, and strumming guitars. A *Newsweek* article of that era called it the "craziest, gayest gathering place in the city." Today it is no longer a scene, but it remains one of New York's most idyllic settings.

   Go down the steps (look at the balustrade's bas-reliefs of the Seasons), and make a right on the path closest to:

12. **The Lake.** Its perimeter pathway lined with weeping willows and Japanese cherry trees, the 22½-acre lake was created from Sawkill Creek, which entered the Park near West 79th Street. The neo-Victorian Loeb Boathouse at the east end of the Lake rents rowboats and bicycles; evenings, you can arrange gondola rides. Along the path

to the Lake, you'll usually see handwriting analysts, masseurs, reflexologists, and other purveyors of New Age services.

Take a Break **The Boathouse Café** (☎ 212/ 517-2233) at the eastern end of the Lake is open from early spring to late October. It offers alfresco lakeside seating on a wooden deck under a white canopy. Overhead heaters allow for the cafe's extended season. The menu is contemporary American, featuring nouvelle pasta dishes, salads, focaccia sandwiches, and heartier entrees such as pan-fried yellowfin tuna with ginger crust. As at Tavern on the Green, the setting is much more of a draw than the food. Lunch and brunch entrees average around $16.

Light fare is served weekdays 9am to 4pm, weekends to 4:30pm; dinner is Wednesday to Friday from 6 to 10pm. A weekend brunch buffet is available from 11am to 3pm.

If you want something simpler and less expensive, the Boathouse complex houses a cafeteria with both indoor and outdoor seating. It serves breakfast and light-fare items year-round. Hours are 9am to 4pm daily in summer; the cafeteria closes a little earlier during the rest of the year.

From the south end of the Boathouse, cross East Drive and follow the path to the:

13. **Conservatory Water.** The above-mentioned Pond and Lake are free-form bodies of water. The Conservatory Water, scene of model boat races (there's even a model boathouse on the Fifth Ave. side where miniature boats are stored), is of formal design. Originally planned as the setting for a conservatory garden (built later and located farther uptown; see stop 18), it is the site of José de Creeft's *Alice in Wonderland* statues (Alice, the Mad Hatter, March Hare, Dormouse, and Cheshire Cat), which were inspired by the John Tenniel illustrations in the original 1865 edition of the book. Overlooking the water is George Lober's Hans Christian Andersen Memorial Statue, complete with an Ugly Duckling. This

gift from Denmark is the setting for storytelling sessions every Saturday from June through September. Circle the pond (*Catcher in the Rye* fans will remember it as the spot where Holden Caufield came to commiserate with the ducks) and peek into the model boathouse if it's open.

Exit the Conservatory Water on the northwest path (past Alice) and continue through Glade Arch, turning left after the 79th Street Transverse and following the path under Greywacke Arch. Ahead on the right, atop the aptly named Vista Rock, is:

14. **Belvedere Castle.** Built by Vaux in 1869, this fanciful medieval-style fortress-in-miniature sits at the highest point in the park and offers sweeping views across Manhattan's verdant playground. To the south, toward the Lake, stretches a wild-by-design tangle of forested trails known as the Ramble, which is fun for exploring by daylight, but dangerous and seedy after dark. The many birds that call this area home led to the creation of a bird-watching and educational center in the Castle's ranger station.

   From Belvedere's balcony, look north over the Delacorte Theater, which in July and August is the setting for the popular **Shakespeare in the Park** series (www.publictheater.org). The series presents a pair of plays in the outdoor theater each summer, performed by both headliner stars (Denzel Washington, Christopher Walken) and eminent Shakespearean thespians (Patrick Stewart did a *Tempest* turn in 1995). Shows start at 8pm, but tickets are free, so it's wise to show up before noon and wait until the Delacorte box office opens at 1pm to snag a pair (you can also get tickets at the Public Theater, on 425 Lafayette St., from 1–3pm). Beyond the Delacorte stretches the Great Lawn, host to some of New York's most famous blowout events, including Paul Simon's gratis concert in the park.

   Just past the Castle and before the Swedish Cottage Marionette Theater (puppet shows July to mid-Aug, Mon–Fri at 10:30am and noon) you'll find the:

15. **Shakespeare Garden,** where the only flowers and plants in evidence are those mentioned in the Bard's plays.

Double back along the 79th Street Transverse to turn left (north) up East Drive (just before Greywacke Arch). Up ahead, across from the backside of the Metropolitan Museums, rises:

16. **The Obelisk (Cleopatra's Needle).** This 3,500-year-old, 77-foot-high, Egyptian pink granite obelisk was a gift to New York City from the khedive of Egypt in 1881 to thank the United States for its help in building the Suez Canal.

Dating from the reign of King Thutmose III in 1600 B.C., the obelisk stood in front of the Temple of the Sun in Heliopolis, Egypt, until the Romans removed it in 12 B.C. and placed it at the approach of a temple built by Cleopatra (hence its nickname). Its hieroglyphics (which are translated here, a gift of Cecil B. de Mille) tell of the deeds of Thutmose III, Ramses II, and Osarkon I. The four bronze crabs peeking out from each corner of the base are 19th-century replicas of the originals, which it is believed were placed there by the Romans as a decorative means of support.

Follow the path behind (west of) the obelisk. When it ends, bear right and follow East Drive, keeping to the left. Soon you'll come to steps and a cast-iron bridge leading to the South Gate House. Make a right onto the jogging path of the:

17. **Reservoir,** created in 1862 to supply New York City's water system. Occupying 106 acres and extending the width of the park, it is surrounded by bridle and jogging paths. The reservoir holds a billion gallons of water, is 40 feet at its greatest depth, and now serves only as an emergency backup water supply. The path around it is 1½ miles long. Walk or jog along the eastern border of the reservoir, getting off at 96th Street (a playground is diagonally across).

Continue north on East Drive to 102nd Street, exit the park, and walk north along Fifth Avenue to the Vanderbilt Gate. This ornate portal, designed in Paris in 1894, formerly graced the Fifth Avenue mansion of Cornelius Vanderbilt II. Fittingly adorned with plant motifs, it is the entrance to the:

18. **Conservatory Garden.** This formal garden was commissioned as a WPA project in 1936. As you enter from
Fifth Avenue, you'll be facing the elegant Italian garden, a
green centered on a classical fountain. It is ringed with
yew hedges and bordered by alleys of Siberian crab apple
trees. In spring, the crab apples bloom with pink and
white flowers, and narcissus grows in the ivy beneath
them.

Walk through the crab apple alley on the left to the
lovely mazelike English garden. You'll find a bronze
statue of the children from the novel *The Secret Garden*
standing in a reflecting pool. In summer, water lilies and
a wide variety of flowering plants and shrubs fill the
garden. Now walk through the Wisteria Pergola (at the
back of the Italian garden). This flower-bedecked,
wrought-iron arbor, especially magnificent in late May,
connects the English and French gardens.

Enter the French garden via rose-covered arched trel-
lises. Two levels of flower beds encircle the Untermeyer
Fountain, which centers on an enchanting sculpture of
dancing maidens by Walter Schott. Here, 20,000 tulips
bloom in spring, and 5,000 chrysanthemums bloom in
fall.

The Upper West Side

Start: 86th Street and Broadway.

Subway: Take the 1 or 9 to 86th Street.

Finish: Lincoln Center.

Time: 3½ hours (allow more time for shopping, refreshment stops, and museum visits).

Best Time: Weekday afternoons, when shops and museums are open but crowds are at a minimum.

The Upper West Side has undergone a decidedly upwardly mobile transformation in the last few decades. Though some magnificent luxury apartment buildings have stood here since the days of gaslights and horse-drawn carriages, they were surrounded by an otherwise unre-markable, largely working-class neighborhood for the first half of the 20th century. Then came Lincoln Center.

A massive urban renewal effort centered around the con-struction of this performing arts complex in the early 1960s. Blocks of dilapidated housing and bodegas gave way to pricey boutiques and exclusive residential buildings.

The Upper West Side

Gentrification almost completely swallowed up the West Side in the decades that followed, but dozens of mom-and-pop dry cleaners and shoe repair shops still remain, giving the West Side its unique flavor. Especially as you go farther uptown, you might spot a neighborhood barber shop still going strong even though a trendy new hair salon has opened nearby, or you'll suddenly come upon a block where the signs are in Spanish and the sounds of salsa blast from everyone's windows.

Some old-timers bemoan the changes, but after the yuppie invasion of the 1970s and 1980s, the West Side has maintained a more democratic and informal atmosphere than the stuffy Upper East Side. The Upper West Side is the neighborhood inhabited by the characters on *Seinfeld* (though most Seinfeldonia, like the diner where they hung out, lies farther uptown from this walk), and it pulses with life. Residents pride themselves on the wonderful food shopping at Fairway and Zabar's and the cheap paperbacks and coffee table art books stacked on the tables of sidewalk entrepreneurs. It's a neighborhood where you can enjoy an authentic Cuban dinner in a simple hole-in-the-wall one night and dine in an elegant French bistro or a sleek sushi bar the next.

● ● ● ● ● ● ● ● ● ● ● ● ● ● ● ● ●

From the 86th Street subway station, walk south down the east side of Broadway to 84th Street ("Edgar Allan Poe Street"). Just off Broadway to your left is:

1. **215 West 84th St.** As recently as the 1840s, this area was still undeveloped rural countryside. Edgar Allan Poe lived briefly with his wife in a farmhouse that stood here on a rocky knoll. He completed his poem "The Raven" here in the summer of 1844.

   Go back to Broadway and cross the street; turn left, heading downtown. At the northwest corner of 80th Street and Broadway stands:

2. **Zabar's** (☎ 212/787-2000), a West Side retail institution. The faint of heart should beware: Zabar's is sheer bedlam, and its crowd of serious shoppers will shove you right out of the way for the perfect wheel of Brie. But plunge into the crowds and wander through the aisles for a mind-boggling selection of imported cheeses, breads,

Kid-Friendly Experiences

- Exploring the American Museum of Natural History (stop 9)
- Relaxing at Strawberry Fields (stop 14)
- Taking in the plaza at Lincoln Center (stop 18)

cold cuts, salads, and appetizers. The aroma of freshly ground coffee pervades the store. At the fish counter, you can get anything from smoked salmon to caviar. If you're taking this tour on a beautiful spring day, you'll find the fixings here for a memorable picnic feast in Central Park.

Don't be daunted either by the long lines you are sure to see emanating from **H&H Bagels,** just across 80th Street. As anyone in the neighborhood will tell you, the bagels here are a favorite front-runner for the coveted title of Best Bagels in New York; they're so fresh that they're still warm from the oven.

Just south of here rises the magnificent 1908 limestone facade of:

3. **The Apthorp,** which commands an entire square block bounded by 78th and 79th streets, Broadway, and West End Avenue. Admire the 1908 building from the Broadway side, standing in front of the stately iron gates that lead into a landscaped central courtyard with a pair of fountains, marble benches, and statuary. You may recognize it from a conga line of New York–based films in which the Apthorp was featured, including *Rosemary's Baby, The Cotton Club, Heartburn, The Money Pit,* and *Network.*

   Turn right and take 78th Street west, heading away from the bustle of Broadway. Then turn left down West End Avenue. At the northeast corner of 77th Street stands the Flemish-style:

4. **West End Collegiate Church and School** (www.west endchurch.org), with dormer windows and a steep, red-tiled roof. The church was built in 1892 for the Collegiate Reformed Protestant Dutch Church, a congregation dating

from the Dutch Nieuw Amsterdam colonists of 1628. The Collegiate School (established in 1638) is one of the oldest independent secondary schools in the country and still functions as one of New York's posh prep schools.

Proceed east on 77th Street back to Broadway and head downtown. At the corner of 75th Street sits **Citarella** (☎ 212/874-0383), another excellent gourmet food shop that in 1997 opened a second floor and began giving Zabar's a run for its money. At 74th Street, you'll pass Fairway, West Siders' favorite produce store. Even in winter, fresh fruits and vegetables abound here, and it's usually a hectic bustle inside. A block farther south, you'll see on the right (though you'll get a better view from stop 6) the splendid beaux arts–style:

5. **Ansonia Hotel,** which is located between 73rd and 74th streets and was built as a luxury residential hotel and completed in 1904. Its architect, W. E. D. Stokes, bought this parcel of land, then surrounded by single-family homes, and decided to raise eyebrows by building a 17-story "tenement" in flamboyant French style. Resembling a lacy, opulent wedding cake, the Ansonia sports a three-story mansard roof and rounded corner towers capped with high domes.

Luxurious apartment houses were all the rage at the turn of the last century, and the Ansonia's early tenants were lured by an incredible list of amenities and services. Messages propelled pneumatically in a network of tubes could be sent from room to room. The Ansonia also contained a grand ballroom, a swimming pool, a trellised roof garden (Stokes kept a small pet bear, goats, and chickens in the roof garden; he sold the eggs to tenants at a discount), a theater, a barber shop, a pharmacist, a florist, and a laundry. Live seals splashed about in the lobby's fountain. Tenants could dine in any of the several restaurants on the premises or have meals sent up to their suites.

The Ansonia has always been a favorite address for musicians, among them Stravinsky, Toscanini, and Caruso. (The apartments here are virtually soundproof, so musicians can practice without fear of disturbing other tenants.)

The golden age of the Ansonia ended with the Great Depression, and the building has slid into a decline marked by legal battles between tenants and owners. It was, however, declared a New York City landmark in 1972. (You may recognize it as the setting for the thriller *Single White Female*.)

☕ **Take a Break** Tucked away in a basement on the downtown side of 72nd Street between Broadway and West End Avenue is a pub that hosts a crowd of neighborhood regulars. The **All State Cafe,** 250 West 72nd St. (☎ **212/874-1883**), serves typical bar food, such as fried calamari, spicy chicken wings, and bowls of chili, plus surprisingly good daily specials. The thick, juicy burgers are among the best in town. If you're there on a chilly winter day, you'll appreciate the fire crackling in the hearth beside the bar. And the jukebox has a great selection of classic rock, jazz, oldies, and swing tunes. The All State is open daily from 11:30am to 1am (later on weekends).

In the early 1970s, this joint was H. M. Tweed's singles bar. On New Year's Day 1973, schoolteacher Roseanne Quinn picked up a guy named John Wayne Wilson and figured he'd make a good 1-night stand. After he strangled and stabbed her, he was arrested, confessed, and committed suicide while awaiting trial. The book and movie inspired by the murder, *Looking for Mr. Goodbar,* became an anthem against the casual sex culture of the '70s.

Go back to Broadway and 73rd Street; now take 73rd Street east and cross Broadway. Between 73rd and 74th streets is the:

6. **Apple Bank,** designed by York and Sawyer in the 1920s and boasting a massive limestone facade and stunning ironwork doors. The structure's trapezoid shape allows it to fill out the plot of land created where Broadway cuts diagonally across Amsterdam Avenue, and its heavy, monumental style is perfectly suited to a bank building. (Be sure to look back across the street at the Ansonia from here.) If you continue walking in this direction, you'll pass beneath a decorative clock, topped with twin lions.

Continue east on 73rd Street to:

7. **Columbus Avenue,** one of New York's trendiest promenades, lined with boutiques, coffee bars, and restaurants. Stores spring up like weeds on Columbus—and they disappear as fast as yesterday's news. Take this part of the stroll to stop and browse in any place that catches your eye. Try **Profiles** (no. 294) and **Kenneth Cole** (no. 353) for up-to-the-minute styles in shoes. **Variazioni** (no. 309) and **Eileen Fisher** (no. 351) sell women's fashions. My favorite shop on this stretch is:

8. **Nancy's Wines for Food,** at no. 313 (☎ 212/877-4040; www.nancyswines.com). Nancy's usually has more than 100 labels of wine in stock under $10, and those that are pricier are generally worth it. Each wine is marked with an index card describing its qualities and what foods it best accompanies. There's no enological snobbery here, just good, plain-spoken advice, excellent wines, and unbelievable prices. Nancy's is open Monday to Thursday 10am to 9pm, Friday and Saturday 10am to 10pm.

While you're meandering up Columbus, take a peek off to your left at 150 West 75th St., where **Anaïs Nin** lived with her mother and brother from 1914 to 1919. In the first-floor rooming house at this address, the teenage writer began penning the diary that became her most important work.

Continue your stroll up Columbus, taking your time to allow for optimum people-watching. At **77th Street,** take a right down a block so admired by Tom Wolfe that he called it "the most beautiful in town" in his book *The Bonfire of the Vanities.* Halfway down it is the entrance to the:

9. **American Museum of Natural History** (☎ 212/769-5100; www.amnh.org), home to 36 million artifacts illustrating the Earth's history. The famous Hall of Dinosaurs, housing several skeletons of those prehistoric creatures, is a perennial hit still basking in the renaissance of dino-interest brought by the *Jurassic Park* film empire. Didactic to the last, the museum labors at many of the high-tech saurian exhibits to gently correct the film's paleontological

errors and other general dinosaur misconceptions. Other highlights include the largest meteorite ever retrieved, which is at the heart of an astounding minerals and gems section; the spanking new, totally rebuilt Rose Center (containing the Hayden Planetarium and IMAX theater); and an impressive collection of pre-Columbian artifacts.

These artifacts bring up a sticky but interesting point: The museum is saddled by tradition to its function, in part, as what should better be termed an ethnology museum. Whole sections devoted here to Haida dugout canoes and totem poles highlight their absence at the Metropolitan and other fine art museums across the park, where European and Mediterranean art and cultural output are displayed. The cultural histories of the "primitive" peoples of the Americas, Africa, and Asia have, under some old racist notion, somehow been relegated here instead, under the museum's category of "natural history." Throughout the museum, plaques, films, and CD-ROM terminals go to great pains to point out the museum's own history of embarrassing errors and to teach that what we consider "scientific fact" is just opinion grounded in the thinking of a particular era.

The suggested admission is worth it; the museum's hours are Sunday to Thursday 10am to 5:45pm, Saturday 10am to 7:45pm (the Rose Center only is also open Fri 10am–8:45pm).

Head back to Columbus Avenue and continue north to **81st Street.** Make a right and head toward Central Park West, passing no. 11, whose apartments are home to actresses Teri Garr and Natassia Kinski. Further ahead on your left, crowning the northwest corner of the intersection, is:

10. **The Beresford,** the first in a long line of architectural gems you'll pass on Central Park West. The Beresford, with its baroque tower and classical ornamentation, is an adaptation of an Italian Renaissance palazzo. Its architect, Emery Roth, was a Jewish immigrant who arrived in this country flat broke as a teenager. He taught himself design and, through sheer hard work and determination, became one of the city's most noted architects.

Apartments at the Beresford are hard to come by and run into the millions of dollars. In 2002, a four-story, 15-room, five-bedroom penthouse was going for a cool $14,950,000 (because, you know, if you break that $15 million mark you just drive off all the bargain hunters). Gangster Meyer Lansky lived here in the 1940s, and more recently, actor Rock Hudson lived here until his death from AIDS in 1985. Other famous residents have included Margaret Mead (who used to walk to work nearby at the Museum of Natural History), Tony Randall, ABC anchor Peter Jennings, his colleague Diane Sawyer, and writer and *Cosmo* Editor in Chief Helen Gurley Brown.

Turn right and head down Central Park West. (Turn back and look up at the Beresford after a half block or so for a better perspective.) Along here is another entrance to the Museum of Natural History, marked by an equestrian statue of Theodore Roosevelt. At the southwest corner of 77th Street and Central Park West, you'll see the:

11. **New-York Historical Society** (☎ 212/873-3400; www.nyhistory.org), a rich repository of artifacts, artworks, and documents that chronicle the city's history. Established in 1804, it is New York's oldest museum. In addition to its renowned research library, the museum's highlights include John James Audubon's original Birds of America watercolor series, a gallery of more than 150 Tiffany lamps, and an extensive collection of early American art. The museum charges admission, and hours are Tuesday to Sunday 11am to 6pm.

From here, cross Central Park West and walk down the park side to better view the buildings we're about to pass. Between 74th and 75th streets stands:

12. **The San Remo,** 145–146 Central Park West. Once home to heavyweight boxing champ Jack Dempsey and pinup idol Rita Hayworth, the San Remo is another grand apartment building bearing the stamp of Emery Roth. The two towers rising at each end are crowned with columned temples. After struggling through the Depression, the owners sold the San Remo and the Beresford together in 1940 for the shocking sum of

$25,000 over the combined mortgages. More recent residents have included actors Dustin Hoffman, Mary Tyler Moore, Bruce Willis and Demi Moore, Diane Keaton, Steve Martin, and popular crooner Barry Manilow.

At Central Park West and 72nd Street is a world-famous architectural masterpiece:

13. **The Dakota,** one of the first luxury apartment buildings in New York, built from 1880 to 1884. Legend has it that the building's name came about when Edward S. Clark, the project's developer, was teased by his friends that the site was so far north of the city center that it might as well be in Dakota territory. Architect Henry J. Hardenbergh, who also designed New York's landmark Plaza Hotel, created a brooding, Germanic structure accented with gables, dormers, and oriel windows, surrounded by a "dry moat." The fortresslike building is so atmospheric that it served as the backdrop to the horror movie *Rosemary's Baby.*

    The list of tenants at this prestigious address has included Lauren Bacall, Leonard Bernstein, Connie Chung, John Madden, Roberta Flack, and Boris Karloff (whose ghost reputedly haunts the halls). But the Dakota will forever be associated with its most famous resident, John Lennon, who was gunned down just outside the building.

    Lennon was returning home to the Dakota after a recording session on December 8, 1980, when he was shot by Mark David Chapman, a lone psychopath who had asked for the former Beatle's autograph only hours earlier. Lennon's widow, Yoko Ono, still lives in the Dakota.

    Just inside the 72nd Street entrance to Central Park lies:

14. **Strawberry Fields,** a memorial to Lennon built and maintained by his widow. The 3-acre teardrop-shaped "international garden of peace" is adorned with more than 150 species of plants (gifts from as many nations) and 2,500 strawberry plants. Near the entrance, a circular black-and-white tile mosaic, a gift from Naples, Italy, spells out the word *Imagine.*

As you exit the park to continue on your route downtown, you'll be right across the street from the:

15. **Majestic Apartments,** 115 Central Park West, another of the grand apartment houses that defines the Central Park West skyline. Until the 12-story Hotel Majestic was built in the 1890s, this site was occupied by wooden shacks and grazing goats. However, it became a sumptuous venue that hosted the likes of Sarah Bernhardt, Edna Ferber, Gustav Mahler, and Vaslav Nijinsky. In 1929, developer Irwin Chanin initiated plans to build a single-tower, 45-story structure. The months that followed, however, saw the stock market crash, so Chanin altered his plans and came up with the 29-story, twin-towered structure you see today between 71st and 72nd streets. He also broke with tradition by scorning the classical European models used for most large residential buildings in New York; instead he chose an adaptation of Art Deco style that he called Modern American. The building was ready for tenants in 1931, but the Depression grew so severe that Chanin had defaulted on his mortgage by 1933.

Although it's had its share of famous residents, including Fred Astaire, Isadora Duncan, and Milton Berle, the Majestic is also connected to two major scandals. Bruno Richard Hauptmann, who was prosecuted for kidnapping the Lindbergh baby, was working as a carpenter here when the crime was committed. A gangland hit took place in the lobby in 1957, when mobster Frank Costello was shot in the head. Fellow gangsters Lucky Luciano and Meyer Lansky also called the Majestic home for a while.

Farther down Central Park West, at the southwest corner of 70th Street, you'll see the neoclassical:

16. **Synagogue of the Congregation Shearith Israel,** which dates from 1897. It's home to the oldest Jewish congregation in the United States, which was founded in 1654 by Sephardic Jews and Spanish and Portuguese immigrants who came to New York via Brazil.

Turn right onto 67th Street, where several buildings contain double-height studio apartments. At no. 1 is the Gothic-style:

17. **Hotel des Artistes,** full of enchanting touches, such as the row of gargoyles below the third-floor windows. Most of the units in the Hotel des Artistes are duplexes and double-height studios. One particularly noteworthy apartment, designed for philanthropist Aaron Naumburg and completed in 1921, has 18-foot ceilings, a wood-balustraded balcony, and lavishly carved woodwork. Naumberg's home was graced with tapestries, fine carpets, antique Italian furniture, paintings, carved figures, and stained-glass windows; it was so spectacular that all the furnishings and artwork were taken as a group to the Fogg Museum in Cambridge and the apartment was re-created as an annex to the museum after Naumberg's death.

The Hotel des Artistes has attracted an astounding number of famous residents, including Rudolph Valentino, Noël Coward, Isadora Duncan, Alexander Woollcott, Edna Ferber, former mayor John Lindsay, former governor Hugh Carey, Norman Rockwell, and Emil Fuchs, portraitist to Queen Victoria. Fuchs, dying of cancer, committed suicide in the Hotel des Artistes in 1929 by shooting himself with a pearl-handled revolver inscribed by Edward VII. More grisliness ensued on December 10, 1929, when bohemian poet Harry Crosby killed both his girlfriend and himself in a ninth-floor apartment.

The ground floor houses the elegant and romantic **Café des Artistes;** peek in the window to see the restaurant's famous wood-nymph murals by Howard Chandler Christy, a longtime tenant in the building. (Some of the models used for the nymphs have returned to dine in the cafe over the years.) Christy's murals and his other depictions of lovely ladies in magazine and book illustrations earned him an invitation to be the sole judge at the first Miss America contest in 1921.

Continue west on 67th Street to Columbus Avenue and make a left. Between 65th and 66th streets stands the **Museum of American Folk Art annex (☎ 212/496-2966;** www.folkartmuseum.org) and its gift shop, stocked with books, jewelry, hand-painted pitchers and vases, prints, and one-of-a-kind greeting cards. Across Broadway, you can't miss:

18. **Lincoln Center** (☎ 212/875-5000; www.lincolncenter.org), the city's premier venue for the performing arts. In 1956, a committee headed by John D. Rockfeller III selected the site for Lincoln Center in what was then a rundown residential area. *West Side Story* was filmed in these streets before an astounding 188 buildings were demolished to clear the area; 1,600 people had to be relocated to make way for the project.

The committee commissioned a group of architects headed by Wallace K. Harrison; each building they created has classical lines and is covered in Italian travertine. The centerpiece of the complex is an outdoor plaza graced with a cafe terrace and a splashing fountain. New Yorkers enjoy free entertainment under the stars here on the plaza in summer, and in December, one of the city's most beautiful Christmas trees is mounted here.

Left of the plaza is **Avery Fisher Hall** (☎ 212/875-5030), with a peristyle of 44 columns soaring seven stories high. It's home to the New York Philharmonic (☎ 212/875-5656; www.newyorkphilharmonic.org), which has counted among its musical directors such luminaries as Zubin Mehta, Arturo Toscanini, Leopold Stokowski, and Leonard Bernstein. On the right side of the fountain is the **New York State Theater** (☎ 212/870-5570), designed by architect Philip Johnson, which hosts performances by the New York City Opera and the New York City Ballet (www.nycballet.com), founded by George Balanchine.

Forming the background of the plaza is the **Metropolitan Opera House** (☎ 212/362-6000; www.metopera.org), which boasts a 10-story marble colonnade. Inside the glass facade, you can see two enormous murals by Marc Chagall. This building is the home of the renowned Metropolitan Opera, one of the most prestigious companies in the world for more than a century; acclaimed stars such as Placido Domingo, Luciano Pavarotti, Jose Carreras, Kathleen Battle, and Marilyn Horne have graced the stage here. In early summer, the Met (as the opera house is commonly known) also hosts the American Ballet Theatre's season. The Met's interior houses seven rehearsal halls and space to store scenery for as many as 15 operas.

The remainder of the complex at Lincoln Center includes the **Guggenheim Bandshell,** used for free outdoor concerts; the **Vivian Beaumont and Mitzi Newhouse Theaters** (☎ 212/239-6200); the **Juilliard School** (☎ 212/799-5000; www.juilliard.edu), the country's premier academy for the performing arts; and **Alice Tully Hall,** home to the Chamber Music Society (☎ 212/875-5788; www.chambermusicsociety.org). Also at Lincoln Center is a branch of the **New York Public Library** (☎ 212/870-1630; www.nypl.org), which serves as both a library and a museum of the performing arts. The library hosts an impressive array of free films and concerts.

One-hour tours of Lincoln Center are offered for a small fee; call ☎ 212/875-5350 to check on the day's tour schedule and to make advance reservations. Calendars of upcoming events, including free concerts, are also available at Lincoln Center and online (see address above).

The Upper East Side

Start: The southeast corner of Central Park, at 59th Street and Fifth Avenue.

Subway: Take the N, R, or W to Fifth Avenue.

Finish: 91st Street and Fifth Avenue.

Time: Approximately 3 hours.

Best Time: Weekday afternoons, when museums and restaurants are open but not as crowded as on Saturdays.

Worst Time: Sundays, when most stores and galleries are closed and the streets seem deserted.

Over a century ago, society watchers predicted that the wealthy and fashionable would settle permanently on the avenues bordering Central Park. Time has proven them right. Fifth Avenue north of Grand Army Plaza, which lies at the southeast corner of the park, is officially called Museum Mile. But the magnificent private mansions built here in the first few decades of the 20th century by some of America's wealthiest industrial tycoons also earned it the title

The Upper East Side

1 Grand Army Plaza
2 The Pierre
3 Knickerbocker Club
4 820 Fifth Ave.
5 The Arsenal
6 3 East 64th St.
7 Home of President Ulysses S. Grant
8 58 East 68th St.
9 680 Park Ave.
10 Union Club
11 East 70th Street
12 Asia Society
13 Hirschl and Adler/
   Knoedler and Company
14 Frick Collection
15 Polo/Ralph Lauren
16 11 East 73rd St.
17 Whitney Museum
   of American Art
18 972 Fifth Ave.
19 Metropolitan Museum of Art
20 Former Home of Jacqueline
   Kennedy Onassis
21 86th Street
22 Guggenheim Museum
23 Cooper-Hewitt National
   Design Museum
24 Convent of the Sacred Heart

of Millionaires' Row. Judging from old photos, it was something to behold.

Today, patrician mansions still stand along the avenue, though others have ceded their coveted real estate to large apartment houses. But the age of imperial living isn't over by any means. Some of the buildings on Fifth Avenue (as well as on Park Ave. and elsewhere on the East Side) contain apartments every bit as palatial and sumptuous as the vanished mansions. Even New Yorkers are surprised to hear of apartments with 20, 30, or even 40 rooms, but they do exist in this neighborhood.

• • • • • • • • • • • • • • • • •

Start your tour where Fifth Avenue and 59th Street meet at:

1. **Grand Army Plaza,** which is adorned with a brilliant gold statue of William Tecumseh Sherman, the ruthless but effective Civil War general who devastated the Southern countryside and brought the civilian population to its knees with the Union army's scorched-earth March to the Sea. "War is cruelty, and you cannot refine it," Sherman once observed, but sculptor Augustus Saint-Gaudens has tried. He's created a classical equestrian statue of the crusty general with a female Winged Victory striding along in front of the horse. It was unveiled on Memorial Day 1903, with bands playing "Marching Through Georgia" and a military parade (some of Sherman's men were among the marchers). This is the patriotic (victorious Union) view of the statue. But truth is in the eye of the beholder, and a popular story goes that a proper Southern lady, upon being told whom the statue represented and the identity of the winged maiden, harrumphed, "Ain't that just like a Yankee, to make the lady walk." If you need sustenance before setting out on your tour, you can hit one of the hot dog carts in the area for a traditional New York lunch on the go.

Now stroll up Fifth Avenue, staying on the park side of the street for the best view of the buildings as you pass. In good weather, bookstalls from The Strand line the sidewalk, full of used volumes at a fraction of the cover price. On the east (right) side of Fifth Avenue, at 61st Street, is:

Kid-Friendly Experiences

This walk isn't really cut out for kids, though they might enjoy the chocolate at Godiva, or playing with the gadgets at Sharper Image. The sometimes oddball art at the modern museums might appeal to some kids, and the Metropolitan (stop 19) has plenty to amuse just about everyone. The Guggenheim (stop 22) and the Whitney Museum (stop 17) may also interest art-loving kids.

2. **The Pierre,** one of Manhattan's priciest and most exclusive hotels since its opening in 1930. In 1932, mystery writer Dashiell Hammett stayed here while working on *The Thin Man,* though, unfortunately, he couldn't pay the bill that he had run up during his stay. He allegedly donned a disguise to sneak out without settling his tab.

   If you're starting out early in the morning, breakfast at the Pierre makes for a pricey but elegant beginning to your tour.

   At the southeast corner of 62nd Street stands the third home of the:

3. **Knickerbocker Club,** which looks a lot like the big private houses that once characterized the avenue. The Georgian brick Knickerbocker, completed in 1915, was the work of a firm called Delano and Aldrich, a favorite of high society in the early 20th century. It retains a very pedigreed image. Ernest Hemingway, looking for peace and quiet, rented an apartment here in 1959 and stayed for about a year.

   The next block up is 63rd Street, and on the east corner you'll see:

4. **820 Fifth Ave.,** one of the earliest apartment houses built hereabouts and still one of the best. Built in 1916, it has only one apartment on each floor, with five fireplaces and seven bathrooms in each one.

   Continue northward on Fifth Avenue to 64th Street. Walk just inside Central Park for a look at:

5. **The Arsenal,** built in 1848 when this neighborhood was distant and deserted. Now housing zoo administration offices, the structure was once a bunkhouse and weapons depot for Civil War troops (notice the railing made of rifles; also see walking tour 8, stop 2). The Central Park Zoo is right behind the building.

Head back onto Fifth Avenue. Opposite the park at the southeast corner of 64th Street (**828 Fifth Ave.**) is the former mansion of coal magnate Edward Berwind.

Head east (away from the park) on 64th Street toward Madison Avenue. This particularly handsome East Side block is lined with architectural extravaganzas. Note in particular:

6. **3 E. 64th St.,** an opulent beaux arts mansion built in 1903 for the daughter of Mrs. William B. Astor. The house was designed by Warren and Wetmore, the firm responsible for Grand Central Terminal, and it now houses the Consulate General of India. Also worthy of admiration on this block are nos. 16, 19 (now home to Wildenstein Gallery open Mon–Fri 10am–5pm), and 20.

At Madison Avenue, turn left and saunter 2 blocks north to 66th Street. Note the rather fantastic apartment house built in 1900 on the **northeast corner of 66th and Madison,** and then turn left (west) off Madison onto 66th Street, heading back toward Fifth Avenue.

Among the many notable houses on this block is the magnificent French Renaissance–style house at **5 E. 66th St.,** with its heavy wooden doors and elegant stonework detail. Built in 1900, it's now home to the Lotos Club, which is dedicated to literature and the fine arts.

Next door, at 3 E. 66th St., is the:

7. **Home of President Ulysses S. Grant,** where he lived from 1881 to 1885. Forced to declare bankruptcy after a disastrous presidency that was marred by scandal, the former Civil War hero retired here to spend his last years penning his memoirs.

Now double back to Madison Avenue, turn left, and continue north for two more blocks, stopping to browse in any of the **boutiques** that catch your eye. There's Nicole Miller; La Perla for lovely lingerie; Emanuel

Ungaro; Godiva, where you can treat yourself to some coffee and a decadent truffle; and Frette for fine Italian linens. At 68th Street, turn right (east) toward Park Avenue. One of the best houses on this block is:

8. **58 E. 68th St.,** on the southwest corner of the intersection with Park Avenue. The house was built in 1919 for Harold J. Pratt, son of Rockefeller partner Charles Pratt.

   Walk to the north side of 68th Street to:

9. **680 Park Ave.,** a neo-Federal town house, built from 1909 to 1911 for banker Percy Rivington Pyne and designed by McKim, Mead, and White. Its style and architecture were copied all along this Park Avenue block. When, from 1948 to 1963, it housed the Soviet Mission to the United Nations, Premier Nikita Krushchev waved to curious crowds from the balcony during his famous shoe-banging visit to the U.N.

   The Marquesa de Cuevas bought 680 Park Ave. in 1965, staving off a slated demolition by presenting it to the **Americas Society** (www.americas-society.org). The society is the only national not-for-profit institution devoted to educating U.S. citizens about their Western Hemisphere neighbors. The society sponsors public art exhibitions and cultural programs on Latin American and Canadian affairs. The other buildings on this block house the Spanish Institute and the Italian Institute.

   Head north on Park Avenue to 69th Street. On the northeast corner stands the:

10. **Union Club,** designed in 1932 to house New York's oldest club. On the other side of 69th Street is Hunter College. Turn right onto 69th Street and continue east toward Lexington Avenue, noting en route **117 E. 69th St.,** a prototypical, not-so-small, private East Side house with beautiful stained-glass panels around the door.

    When you arrive at Lexington Avenue, detour right a few steps to a still-operating branch of **Shakespeare and Co.** (no. 939; www.shakeandco.com), Manhattan's famously literary bookseller whose West Side main branch was put out of business in 1996 when Barnes and Noble strategically built two megastores within walking distance. Double back up Lexington 1½ blocks uptown to 70th Street. Turn left and head back toward Park Avenue along:

11. **70th Street,** which presents a succession of elegant houses, each more beautiful than the next. Some consider this the finest street in New York. Note in particular no. 125, a post–World War II mansion built for Paul Mellon in a French provincial style.

    When you arrive at the Park Avenue end of the block, note the modern building on the northeast corner, which houses the:

12. **Asia Society** (☎ 212/288-6400 or 212/517-ASIA; www.asiasociety.org). The Asia Society offers workshops, lectures, films, and performances on Asian culture. Major art exhibitions, both ancient and contemporary, are held in the galleries; an admission fee is charged. The museum is open Tuesday through Thursday and Saturday 11am to 6pm, and Friday 11am to 9pm.

    Cross Park Avenue and note **720 Park Ave.** on the northwest corner of the intersection. This building is a prime example of the sort of swanky, enormous apartment building that lured former mansion dwellers away from their private houses. The upper stories of buildings like no. 720 often contain apartments with three or four floors and dozens of rooms.

    Continue on East 70th Street, crossing Madison, toward Fifth Avenue. Two of the Upper East Side's premier art galleries are along 70th Street.

13. **Hirschl and Adler** (☎ 212/535-8810; www.hirschl andadler.com), at no. 21, shows quality American and European art, from 18th-century to current day masterpieces, in many media. Over five floors, various galleries cover everything from American decorative arts to modern art (including Southern black folk artist Forrest Bess, Cy Twombly, Joseph Beuys, performing artist team Gilbert and George, John Moore, and Fairfield Porter), American prints to the big old guns, from John Singleton Copley, Winslow Homer, Edward Hopper, and Georgia O'Keeffe to Mary Cassatt, Picasso, Matisse, and Renoir.

    Next door, at no. 19, is **Knoedler and Company** (☎ 212/794-0550; www.knoedlergallery.com), a major gallery for established American artists such as Helen Frankenthaler, Adolph Gottlieb, Nancy Graves, Frank Stella, and John Walker.

Nearing Fifth Avenue, you'll pass a lovely courtyard and lily pond, surrounded by stately black iron gates, before reaching the entrance to my favorite New York museum, the:

14. **Frick Collection** (☎ **212/288-0700;** www.frick.org), housed in the 1914 mansion of steel magnate Henry Clay Frick and very evocative of the Gilded Age. The beautiful classic garden overlooking 70th Street was built in 1977. Frick always intended that his art collection be opened to the public after his death. The works are arrayed in rooms, many with Frick's original furnishings, centered around a small, plant-filled atrium with classical styling, a vaulted skylight, and a softly splashing fountain. If you have time for only one museum on this tour, the modestly sized but rich Frick Collection may be your best choice.

The collections range from Italian medieval (a panel from Duccio's *Maestà*) and the Renaissance (Piero della Francesca, Bellini, Bronzino, Titian, and El Greco), to later French, Spanish, Flemish, German, and American masterpieces from the likes of Rembrandt, Ingres, Gainsborough, Boucher, Goya, Whistler, Degas, and Monet. Fragonard's racy rococo *The Progress of Love* series is installed in a vestibule. Also, don't miss Hans Holbein the Younger's pair of incisive portraits of rivals Thomas Cromwell and Sir Thomas More.

The Frick Collection is open Tuesday to Saturday 10am to 6pm (to 9pm Fri, with a cash wine bar after 6:30pm), and Sunday 1 to 6pm. Admission is charged, and no children under 10 are admitted (children from ages 10–16 must be accompanied by an adult).

Turn right at the corner of Fifth Avenue, passing a beautiful colonnade on the side of the Frick building. Continue 2 blocks north, and turn right onto 72nd Street, heading toward Madison Avenue. On your left, at no. 9, is the **Lycée Français** (a French primary and secondary school), housed in an elaborate 1894 building of the late French Renaissance style. At the southeast corner of 72nd Street and Madison is:

15. **Polo/Ralph Lauren.** This showcase store, housed in a renovated mansion that dates from 1895, looks for all the world like an English country mansion inside, complete with working fireplaces, Persian rugs, antiques, and a grand baronial staircase. The store is closed on Sundays.

    Take Madison Avenue up a block to 73rd Street, passing **The Sharper Image** (no. 900), the catalog store for the gadget-hound in all of us, and **Yumi Katsura** (no. 907), a boutique showcasing exquisite wedding gowns for the well-to-do bride. Detour to your left on 73rd Street to see:

16. **11 E. 73rd St.,** a particularly sumptuous house built in 1903 by McKim, Mead, and White for Joseph Pulitzer, the Hungarian-born publisher of a once-famous but long-vanished newspaper called the *New York World.* Pulitzer rarely lived in this house because of his extreme sensitivity to sound. At one time, it contained a special sound-proofed room (mounted on ball bearings, no less) to prevent vibrations. When he died in 1911, Pulitzer bequeathed $2 million to the Columbia Graduate School of Journalism, whose trustees bestow the Pulitzer Prize awards for outstanding achievement in journalism, literature, drama, and musical composition.

    Retrace your steps back to Madison Avenue and turn left. At the southeast corner of 75th and Madison you'll see the:

17. **Whitney Museum of American Art** (☎ 212/570-3676; www.whitney.org), housed in a 1966 architectural masterpiece by Marcel Breuer. The Whitney contains an impressive collection of 20th-century American art, with paintings that reflect trends from naturalism to pop art and abstract expressionism. Roy Lichtenstein, Georgia O'Keeffe, Edward Hopper, and Jasper Johns are just a few of the artists represented here. Hours are Tuesday to Thursday and Saturday to Sunday 11am to 6pm, Friday 1 to 9pm. An admission fee is charged.

    ☕ **Take a Break** In the museum's basement, **Sarabeth's at the Whitney** (☎ 212/570-3670) is much more than your average museum cafeteria—and more expensive, with dishes starting at $13.50 and brunches starting at $6.75. You can't go wrong with Sarabeth's delightful velvety cream-of-tomato soup. Sarabeth's is also famous for its scrumptious desserts. Brunch (served Sat–Sun) is known for its extensive choices. It's open Tuesday to Thursday 11am to 4:30pm, Friday 11am to 3:45pm, and Saturday and Sunday 10am to 4:30pm.

Though it's housed in the museum, you don't have to pay to reach the cafe; just pick up a free pass at the main ticket desk (you can bypass the museum admissions line).

Leave the museum and continue uptown on Madison Avenue. Past 76th Street, you'll pass one of New York's grand old hotels, **The Carlyle,** which has counted two presidents (Harry Truman and John F. Kennedy) among its famous guests. The west side of Madison Avenue from 76th to 77th streets is lined with a procession of intriguing contemporary art galleries, including the **Gagosian Gallery** (www.gagosian.com) in the penthouse of no. 980 (20th-century artists, including Frank Stella, Richard Serra, Andy Warhol, Mark di Suervo, Chris Burden, and Walter de Maria) and **David Findlay** (www.davidfindlay galleries.com) at no. 984 (19th- and 20th-century American and European art).

Turn left when you reach 79th Street and return to Fifth Avenue. The impressive row of buildings includes everything from French château-style structures to neo-Georgian town houses. When you reach the corner of Fifth Avenue, turn left for a look at:

18. **972 Fifth Ave.,** between 78th and 79th streets. It is now the French Embassy's Cultural Services Office, but it was built in 1906 as a wedding present for Payne Whitney by his doting (and childless) rich uncle, Oliver Payne, a Civil War officer and one of the benefactors who helped to found Cornell's Medical College. This McKim, Mead, and White opus cost $1 million and was the talk of the town in its day. Step inside for a glance at its neoclassical rotunda. The broken statue on the central pedestal caused quite a stir in 1995 when a passing art historian pegged it as a long-lost work by Renaissance master Michelangelo.

For years having served as a fountain spout, the suddenly famous Cupid (or, depending on whom you ask, young Apollo or a young archer) sculpture was spirited away for a world tour while the controversy over its attribution raged. Some say Michelangelo's teacher Bertoldo sculpted it; others claim that it's a 19th-century fake.

Next door, on **the corner of 78th Street,** is the classic French-style mansion of tobacco millionaire James B. Duke (as in Duke University). His daughter Doris occupied the house intermittently until 1957, when she donated it to New York University. NYU now operates it as a fine arts institute.

Now turn around and walk north on Fifth Avenue. On your left at 82nd Street is the grand entrance to the:

19. **Metropolitan Museum of Art** (☎ 212/535-7710; www.metmuseum.org), one of the world's greatest cultural institutions. The block of 82nd Street that faces the museum's mammoth staircase acts as a sort of formal court. The Met's collection is enormous—the largest in the Western Hemisphere—and includes an Egyptian wing that boasts tens of thousands of objects. Its Temple of Dendur, circa 15 B.C., from Lower Nubia, was shipped piece by piece to the Met and painstakingly reconstructed. It would take a lifetime to see all of the Met's treasures, so it might be best to save it for another day and admire the exterior for now.

Museum hours are Sunday and Tuesday to Thursday 9:30am to 5:15pm, Friday and Saturday 9:30am to 8:45pm. There's a hefty suggested admission price.

Continue uptown past 85th Street. The building at 1040 Fifth Ave. was for many years the:

20. **Home of Jacqueline Kennedy Onassis.** After her first husband's assassination, she moved here so that Caroline could attend school at nearby Sacred Heart. The former first lady adored New York and was often spotted strolling nearby in her beloved Central Park. After her death from cancer in 1994, hundreds of mourners gathered outside this building, many leaving flowers on the sidewalk in her memory.

Continue uptown to:

21. **86th Street.** The brick and limestone mansion on the southeast corner of Fifth Avenue and 86th Street was built in 1914 for William Star Miller, but was more famously the home of Grace Vanderbilt, once known as the queen of America's high society. Born Grace Graham Wilson, she was the daughter of a Southern Civil War profiteer who moved north and carefully stitched his family into New York high society. She was first engaged to the Vanderbilt's eldest son, William Henry II, but he died in 1892. Then she was betrothed to Cecil Baring—until Baring Bank crashed in 1893 and she broke it off. It's no wonder, then, that the Vanderbilts sniffed a golddigger in the socialite, and when their now-eldest son and heir-apparent Cornelius III became engaged to her as well, they promptly refused their permission. When the younger Cornelius still would not relent, his father disinherited him as primary heir. Cornelius III's brothers were more forgiving, however, and redistributed the inheritance more equally than the will called for after their father's death.

The intelligent Cornelius III went on to grow his wealth through his love of science—he was a consulting engineer on New York's first subway system—and Grace became the primary New York hostess for almost every visiting monarch and merchant-prince. They moved into a mansion at 640 Fifth Ave., built in the 1880s by Cornelius III's grandfather William Henry I, which was located down on 51st Street and was the first of a concentration of family houses that at the turn of the 20th century caused Fifth Avenue to be called "Vanderbilt Alley." Despite losing over $8 million in the Great Crash of 1929, the Vanderbilts foolishly maintained their lavish lifestyle throughout the Depression. By the end of the 1930s they were, for Vanderbilts, nearly broke (by which I mean they only had $4 million to spare). They had also become pretty much isolated down around 51st Street, surrounded by ghosts of the Vanderbilt past, lots of noisy traffic, and the new office buildings that had replaced many of the other Millionaire's Row mansions done in by the Depression. Grace and her husband ended up having to sell the 640 Fifth Ave. house, and Cornelius III died in

1942. Grace retreated to this 86th Street address in 1944, but the exile appears, at least from the look of this house, to have been comfortable.

Two blocks farther up Fifth Avenue is the unmistakable:

22. **Guggenheim Museum** (☎ 212/423-3500; www. guggenheim.org), between 88th and 89th streets, whose building piques just as much interest as the collection of 19th- and 20th-century masterpieces it houses. Designed by Frank Lloyd Wright in 1959, it set off a storm of architectural controversy when it was built. Nowadays, New Yorkers have grown to think of the building as a treasured landmark. The structure has a unique spiral shape; visitors generally take an elevator to the top floor, and then walk down the ramp, viewing the works of art hung along the curved walls that include many special exhibitions along with works by Brancusi, Alexander Calder, Marc Chagall, Kadinsky, Paul Klee, Joan Miró, Mondrian, Picasso, and van Gogh.

The Guggenheim's hours are Sunday to Wednesday 9am to 6pm, Friday and Saturday 9am to 8pm. Admission is charged. Check out the museum store's T-shirts, gifts, prints, and books.

Uptown from the Guggenheim, between 90th and 91st streets, is another major sight, the:

23. **Cooper-Hewitt National Design Museum** (☎ 212/ 849-8400; www.si.edu/ndm). Under the auspices of the Smithsonian Institution, this museum is housed in the former Andrew Carnegie mansion. Built in 1901, this Georgianesque palace originally shared the neighborhood with squatters' shanties and roaming pigs. By the time the squatters were gone and the streets were built up with fine houses, Carnegie was dead. His widow lived in the house until 1949. The museum, with its changing design exhibits, is open Tuesday 10am to 9pm, Wednesday to Friday 10am to 5pm, Saturday 10am to 6pm, and Sunday noon to 6pm; admission is charged.

Across 91st Street from the main entrance to the Cooper-Hewitt is the:

24. **Convent of the Sacred Heart Girls' School,** occupying what was once the largest private house ever built in Manhattan. Financier Otto Kahn bought the property from Andrew Carnegie in 1913, and construction of his mansion, which was modeled on the papal chancellery in Rome, was completed in 1918. Other houses on this 91st Street block, notably nos. 7 and 9, are almost as grand.

Take 91st Street east to Madison Avenue and turn right (downtown) if you'd like to end the tour with a pick-me-up.

Winding Down At the southwest corner of Madison Avenue and 91st Street is **Jackson Hole** (☎ 212/427-2820). Many New Yorkers argue that Jackson Hole flips the best burgers in the city, and you certainly get a lot for your money (burgers start at $6.25). In addition to juicy burgers, Jackson Hole offers omelets, honey-dipped fried chicken, sandwiches, salads, and great desserts. Open daily.

Morningside Heights & Harlem

Start: 110th Street and Broadway.
Subway: 1, 9 to Cathedral Parkway (110th St.)
Finish: 125th Street.
Time: Approximately 4 hours.
Best Time: Wednesdays (for Amateur Night at the Apollo Theater).

Harlem's not just a neighborhood, it's a whole separate city. No, seriously. The Dutch founded two cities on this isle between the East River and the Hudson River. The first of those early Dutch colonies was Nieuw Amsterdam, down in the tip of Manhattan and bounded by the wall of Wall Street, with farmland north of the city walls ("farm" in Dutch is *bouwerie,* and the Bowery district was once just that).

Morningside Heights & Harlem

1 Peace Fountain
2 Cathedral of St. John the Divine
3 Columbia University
4 St. Paul's Chapel
5 Sculpture Garden
6 Wallach Art Gallery
7 The Columbia School of Journalism
8 Barnard College
9 Riverside Church
10 Grant's Tomb
11 Jewish Theological Seminary
12 Teacher's College
13 Morningside Park
14 Malcolm Shabazz Mosque No. 7
15 Malcolm Shabazz Harlem Market
16 Mount Morris Historic District
17 Marcus Garvey Park
18 Doctor's Row
19 Hale House
20 125th Street
21 Studio Museum
22 55 W. 125th St.
23 Apollo Theater

Subway ⓜ   Take a Break ☕

In 1658, way up the East River, where the island of Manhattan started narrowing and an Indian village once lay, the Dutch founded a separate town called Nieuw Harlem. It took quite a while for the two communities, New York and New Harlem, to grow together and fuse into one city (it didn't help matters that someone tossed a big old park in between the two). In 1837, the railroad brought development to this sleepy town of just over 200 residents, but it also created the squalor of a factory-and-warehouse neighborhood. The farms disappeared, and Irish immigrants arrived in droves looking for places to squat for free.

East Harlem, its landscaped slashed by still more railroad lines in the 1880s, never grew out of its bottom-of-the-economic-ladder, working-class roots as successive waves of the most downtrodden citizens called it home: Russians, Italians, Irish, Hungarians, Scandinavians, Spaniards, Jews, and eventually Puerto Ricans.

The core of Harlem slowly became a middle class neighborhood. A largely German population built the family brownstones and row houses that line many of Harlem's streets to this day. When the IRT subway line extended up here in 1901, immigrants from the crowded Lower East Side poured into this neighborhood of lower rents and more space, and by 1917 Harlem had some 170,000 Jewish residents. This crashed the housing market, and when the Jews moved on, the city's impoverished and oppressed black community saw a great opportunity to secure excellent housing at low cost and moved in.

This changeover in the neighborhood's makeup dovetailed nicely with the opening up of the country after the Civil War. More and more black sharecroppers left the South and workers sailed up from the Caribbean, all looking for a better life. As with almost every immigrant group in the first 3 decades of the 20th century, when you wanted to find those streets paved with gold, New York City was the place to go—and the place to live in New York, if you were black, was Harlem.

From 1920 to 1930, Harlem's black population swelled from 83,000 to almost 204,000, and began brewing up a distinctive cultural revitalization that became known as the Harlem Renaissance. W. E. B. Du Bois encouraged his African brothers and sisters to explore their own culture and expand their intellect. Harlem's creative geniuses responded in force. Langston Hughes penned his poetry and Eubie Black and Noble Sissle wrote plays (in which Florence Mills acted). William H. Johnson and Aaron Douglas painted while Cab Calloway and Duke Ellington headlined at the (whites-only) Cotton Club. Marcus Garvey started telling blacks it was okay to be proud of their heritage.

The stock market crash of 1929 and the ensuing Great Depression snuffed out the Harlem renaissance. It must be remembered that the theaters, concert halls, and other venues were almost entirely white-owned. Black Harlem may have created its own renaissance, but it was the whites who pro-fited from it. As poet Langston Hughes put it: "The ordinary negro hadn't heard of the Negro Renaissance. And if they had, it hadn't raised their wages any." The thirties were rough all over the U.S., but Harlem residents got through these tough times by creating a close-knit community.

Tensions in the city were running high after the Depression, and race riots began in 1935. After World War II, African-American culture turned its eyes once again to Harlem as Malcolm X and other Muslim ministers began preaching in the mosques that suddenly began popping up around Harlem. Tensions increased, and race riots plagued Harlem throughout the 1960s.

Things didn't really get better for Harlem with the new Civil Rights movement of the late 1960s. The neighborhood just got poorer and poorer, the landlords more corrupt, the people more dispirited, the gangs rougher. In some parts, Harlem looked like a Third World shantytown. So much was abandoned, boarded up, burned-out, squatted in, and half-ruined, and so many landlords were eventually caught as tax cheats, that by the end of the 1970s the city found itself in ownership of about 65% of the neighborhood. And, shame on them, it took them almost 30 years to do something useful to turn the area around.

By the mid-1990s, Harlem was still in a pitiful state. When compared to the rest of NYC, it had nearly twice the unemployment and a 20% lower median income. A combina-tion of poor sanitation, lack of health care, gang violence, and disease epidemics such as AIDS gave Harlem a death rate *five times* the city's average—and those are 1997 figures!

But 1997 was perhaps the nadir of Harlem's troubles. In the years since, it has started on a remarkable turnaround. Millions in investments and seed money have been poured into the area to jump-start local businesses. Housing plans have rehabilitated row houses and created lower income co-ops and apartments (replacing those awful projects). New shopping centers are opening up every year, cultural institutions are mushrooming across the landscape, and galleries are popping up. What's more, middle class folks from outside the neighborhood have already begun shopping for bargains on homes that would cost three to five times as much if they were just a dozen or 2 blocks farther south (though not for long).

This is a neighborhood of gorgeous (if often decaying) brownstones and row houses, of busy barbershops and nail salons where old friends pass the day in good company, of street markets and wide, slightly desolate boulevards, of tiny crowded restaurants and of more churches than you could shake a crucifix at—not to mention temples, mosques, and other houses of worship that make up the devout bouillabaisse of Harlem's mixed community.

One of my favorite things about walking around Harlem has to be the chance to sit down and dig into a plate piled high with soul food—succulent fried chicken, sticky-fingers barbecue, slightly spiced mac and cheese, mashed potatoes with gravy, black-eyed peas, collard greens, grits, hush puppies, sweet potato pie, and spoon bread.

Many people associate Harlem with African Americans, but as we've seen, that wasn't always the case, and it still isn't entirely accurate. The whole of East Harlem is better known as "the Barrio"—or, if you're partial to song lyrics, "Spanish Harlem"—one of the largest Latino neighborhoods in the city, and Italian Harlem still exists around 116th St. and Pleasant Avenue. Heck, there's even a sliver of Harlem that's traditionally Irish Catholic (I've never found it, but comedian-philosopher George Carlin claims to have grown up there). The recent influx of bargain-hunting downtowners and cash-strapped Columbia grads who fail to move away after graduation have brought more white faces to the urban mix in these streets (especially to those below 116th). These days, Harlem is seeing a degree of racial integration that surely would bring a smile to Dr. King's face.

That said, for a century now, the bulk of Harlem has been black, its overarching identity African American, and it's that culture, history, and monuments that make this walk interesting.

Fair warning: once we leave Morningside Heights with its cathedrals and colleges, and cross into Harlem proper, this will not always be the prettiest of walks. Much of the neighborhood is still struggling out of its old urban slum identity of gutted buildings and an oppressed, impoverished populace. There are plenty of "development corporations" and offices devoted to helping out new businesses, but alas they are outnumbered by the boarded-up brownstones, abandoned apartment buildings, and derelict store-fronts. The neighborhood still has a long way to go.

So, yes, Harlem is a neighborhood in flux, undergoing its biggest change since the civil rights era. However, to my mind this only makes it all the more exciting to wander, to explore, to dig into the soul food (mmm . . . soul food), and to witness firsthand this second Harlem renaissance.

Our walk actually doesn't start in Harlem, but in the neighboring district called Morningside Heights, perched atop a cliff between Harlem and the Hudson. The land was too steep and rocky and isolated to be developed and long remained largely drowsy farmland (along with the usual insane asylum and orphanage). Then 1880 brought Riverside Drive, the Eighth Avenue El, and the developers. Still, it remains a somewhat more stately and wide-open area of Manhattan, defined by institutes of learning (Columbia University, Barnard College, the Union and Jewish Theological Seminaries, Teacher's College) and gargantuan houses of worship (St. John the Divine and Riverside Church).

Note: You could very easily make this into two shorter walks, one of Morningside Heights, the other of Harlem (just grab the 2 or 3 subway to 116th St. and Amy Ruth's for the Harlem section of the tour).

• • • • • • • • • • • • • • •

From the 110th street subway stop, walk east on Cathedral Parkway (aka 110th St.), noting the funky gargoylish stone braces under the lower level windows of no. 527 on the left. Turn left up Amsterdam Avenue to our first stop and a nip of bracing brew.

Starting Out **Hungarian Café,** 1030 Amsterdam Ave. (☎ 212/866-4230), is popular with Columbia students for its scrumptious Eastern European pastries, Vienna-style coffee, and lethal rum balls. This simple, delightfully dingy cafe also has some tables out on the sidewalk looking across the street to our first stop, the:

1. **Peace Fountain,** built in 1985 by Greg Wyatt, the fountain is a pile of swirling bronze with Michael the archangel sticking it to Satan atop a double-helix pedestal of DNA. Weird. Much more charming is the ring encircling the fountain, a series of animals dancing along the rail to meet at a large Noah's Arc, all of them molded by middle and high schoolers. Surrounding the fountain are booklike plaques of educators, writers, musician, philosophers, and other cultural heroes, while beyond, in the park, a 40-foot-high, neo-Gothic, 1916-vintage **Outdoor Pulpit** stands forlornly with only a wandering, bedraggled, and much-photographed peacock to keep it company.

Next door is the unmistakable bulk of:

2. **The Cathedral of St. John the Divine** (☎ 212/316-7540; www.stjohndivine.org). For those of you doing the math on your fingers and wondering how NYC can have two cathedrals (St. Patrick's and St. John's) the answer is: Episcopalians. St. Paddy's is Catholic. St. John's has the better organ. Oh, and at 121,000 square feet, it's also the largest Gothic-style church in the entire world (take *that,* Europe). At 146 feet wide, it's twice as broad as

Kid-Friendly Experiences

- Chowing down at Amy Ruth's (see the "Take a Break" box on p. 188)
- Exploring Morningside Park (stop 13)
- Picking up some souvenirs at Malcolm Shabazz Harlem Market (stop 15)

Westminster, the roof towers 177 feet above the ground, and its record-breaking length of 601 feet led to the quip that it would fit "Two football fields, end to end, with room left for the football."

It actually wasn't supposed to be Gothic at all. The original architects drew up plans for a structure in the then-fashionable neo-Romanesque style, but between the 1887 purchase of the land, the 1892 ceremonial laying of the cornerstone, and 1911 when the choir was finally put in place, the old plan was chucked and Ralph Adams Cram came in with his own grandly Gothic ideas. The cathedral had its formal debutante party on November 30, 1941. One week later, the Japanese bombed Pearl Harbor and World War II put a halt to construction, which continued fitfully thereafter.

By 1967, the church decided to start pouring funds into helping the community, and it wasn't until 1978 that they started raising the cash to continue the masonry. By 1992, with just 50 feet of the first tower completed, work pretty much halted, with most of the building funds going to preserving the raw, half-finished structure (though they did continue to carve the statuary around the main door, completed in 1997). Many despair that, in this secular age, it will never be completed, but as Ed Koch pointed out way back in 1979, "I am told that some of the great cathedrals took over five hundred years to build. But I would like to remind you that we are only in our first hundred years." So New York's well ahead of the scheduling curve on cathedral building.

That church houses some fantastic artistic treasures among its thematic chapels (dedicated to sports, poetry, patriotism, law, medicine, firefighting, conservation, and more). The stone bones of the piers and crossing may be delightfully raw, rough, and half-finished, but the decorations went ahead full steam.

There are two sets of Renaissance-era tapestries. The Mortlake Tapestries in the chapels were woven in 1623 on English looms, but the design—the acts of the Apostles—was actually a commission from Pope Leo X to Renaissance titian Raphael, who drew up the original sketches. Hanging above the choir, the Barberini Tapestries are also from the

17th century, this time depicting scenes from the Life of Christ and woven in Cardinal Barberini's papal tapestry factory.

The rose window, 50 feet across if it's an inch, is composed of 10,000 pieces of colored glass, and that Christ figure in the center is life-sized (assuming Jesus was tall for his era, at 5 ft., 7 in.). The 61 silver trumpets ranked below it belong to the Ernest M. Skinner organ, 8,035 pipes put together in 1910 (it got an overhaul and a new stop in 1954, but otherwise is an original).

Head into the ambulatory (the hallway that wraps around the choir and back behind the altar) from the left aisle. The third chapel (St. Columba) and the fourth, or central chapel (St. Savior's) are both prefaced by arched of statues carved by Gutzon Borglum, who did a pretty good job considering this is relatively teensy compared to the scale he was used to (he's the guy who used blasting caps to sculpt Mt. Rushmore's giant presidential noggins).

Inside the Savior's Chapel is a 600-pound bronze altarpiece coated in white gold leaf and depicting the *Life of Christ* (1990) finished by Keith Haring one month before he succumbed to AIDS. In the sixth chapel (St. Ambrose's) is a statue of St. Anthony by the Italian Renaissance master of glazed terra-cottas, Luca della Robbia.

St. John the Divine is open Monday to Saturday 7:30am to 6pm, and Sunday 7:30am to 7pm. Admission is $2. There are $3 tours Tuesday to Saturday at 11am, Sunday at 1pm.

Exit the cathedral from the front door and continue north on Amsterdam Avenue. On your right as you continue walking is the expansive bulk of **St. Luke's Hospital,** bits of the original (1890s) beaux arts architecture by Ernest Flagg still visible amid the modern accretions. At 116th Street, turn left onto the campus of:

3. **Columbia University** (☎ 212/854-4900; www.columbia.edu), an illustrious member of the Ivy League. Columbia's profs and alumns have earned 64 Nobel Prizes in various disciplines, and it has matriculated the likes of Enrico Fermi, Allen Ginsburg, Jack Kerouac (okay, so he dropped out), Art Garfunkel, Langston Hughes, Lauryn

Hill (another dropout), Martha Stewart (hey, I only specified "famous"), and Paul Robeson, with a faculty ranging from John Dewey to Franz Boas. One past university president, Dwight D. Eisenhower, only left his tenure (1948–53) in order to pursue the White House.

Columbia's sprawling city campus—covering 7 blocks, from 114th to 120th streets, between Amsterdam and Broadway—is the world's largest collection of McKim, Mead & White buildings. Charles Follen McKim designed the lot in Italianate style but on the plan of Athens's Agora, where strolling philosophers once taught young toga-clad apprentice thinkers. This wasn't the school's first home, however.

King George II granted New York City a royal charter for a school in 1754. At that time the college was called, naturally, "King's College." The school changed its name to "Columbia" in 1784, after the American Revolution. As King's College, the school matriculated the likes of Alexander Hamilton and John Jay, the first Supreme Court Chief Justice (they've since churned out six more), and in 1767 the very first medical doctors were granted degrees in America.

In 1814, the state gave the college a lot of useless, weed-ridden, rock-filled land way up north of the city, around Fifth Avenue in the unpopular zone between 47th and 51st streets. In 1857 the college moved uptown to a 49th Street address before making the final move here to Morningside Heights in 1897 to occupy the former site of an insane asylum. In the meantime, Columbia held on to that worthless plot of midtown land, leasing it out in 1928 to a developer named John D. Rockefeller Jr. In 1985, the university finally sold the land to its tenant, Rockefeller Center, for $400 million in the single biggest real estate deal in New York history.

From the group of eight young men first taught by Samuel Johnson in July 1754 in the schoolhouse at Trinity Church downtown, by 2001 the school had grown to an enrollment of 22,892, of which only around 7,000 were undergrads—the bulk of enrollment is in the graduate and professional colleges of journalism, medicine, architecture, nursing, law, engineering, social work, and business. Of course the habit of teaching only "young men" took a while to kick—try 1983, when the first women were admitted, making Columbia the last Ivy League school to pull its head out of the sand on this issue by a good number of years.

The pedestrianized bit of 116th Street that you're walking on is called College Walk. Saunter up to its center, to your left (south), across a lawn below you, stretches the facade of Butler Hall, one of the largest libraries in America, boasting more than five million volumes (there's a rare book and manuscript section up on the sixth floor that hosts regular exhibits). To your right, dominating the campus, is the impressive rotunda of **Low Memorial Library,** modeled vaguely after Rome's Pantheon and named to honor the father of one of Columbia's greatest presidents, Seth Low (the guy who moved the college up here before becoming an NYC mayor). Walk up the steps, around the right side of Low, and on your right you'll see:

4. **St. Paul's Chapel,** cute as a button and at least twice as majestic, a vaguely neo-Byzantine "churchlet" built of brick (laid in a quirky herringbone pattern) and brick-like tiles in the dome, all the brainchild of Howells & Stokes from 1904 to 1907. They sponsor a concert series Tuesdays at 6pm, Fridays at 8pm (☎ **212/854-0480;** www.columbia.edu/cu/earl/music_schedule.htm).

Upon exiting the chapel from the front door, turn left then left again to walk down the chapel's right side, past a small grove of chestnut trees on your right where a cast of Rodin's *Thinker* ponders the passing students. Continue up a small pedestrian bridge into a neat little:

5. **Sculpture Garden** on a brick terrace suspended above Amsterdam Avenue. Among the modern works poised on pedestals are Henry Moore's globular 1967 *Three Way Piece: Points,* Gertrude Schweitzer's balancing act of bodies called *Flight* (1981), and a massive, typically lumpy Lipchitz work glowering atop the entrance to the modern Law School called *Bellerophon Taming Pegasus.* It was installed in 1977, is 30 by 28 feet, and weighs 23 tons (looks it, too).

Double back over the pedestrian bridge and past the chapel to turn right, past Avery Hall to Schermerhorn Hall, which houses the:

6. **Wallach Art Gallery,** founded in 1986 and presenting a rotating series of exhibitions of contemporary art throughout the academic year (check out www.columbia. edu/cu/wallach for information). It's open Wednesday to Saturday 1 to 5pm.

Exiting Schermerhorn, go back toward Avery Hall but veer right, past the double-loop sculpture *Curl* (1968 by Celment Meadmore), then left to walk down the far side of Low and back onto College Walk. Turn right onto it, then divert left to walk around to the entrance to:

7. **The Columbia School of Journalism,** one of the top two journalism schools in the country (the other's also in Columbia—Missouri), founded in 1912 by publishing mogul Joseph Pulitzer. The school is in charge of award-ing the annual prestigious Pulitzer Prize for journalism. A 1914 statue of Thomas Jefferson by alumnus William Ordway Partridge frowns from the top of the steps to the school.

Continue along College Walk to pop off campus onto Broadway and turn right. On your left, you're passing the closed campus of:

8. **Barnard College,** a women's college and one of the prestigious "seven sisters" schools. Columbia University's rather enlightened 10th president, Frederick Barnard, who spent his tenure from 1864 to 1883 convincing the trustees to set up a course for women, established Barnard. Of course, because women weren't allowed on campus, and professors weren't allowed to talk to them in any event, the course didn't really take off, but by 1889 they'd worked out the kinks by founding a whole college just for the ladies across the street, and naming it Barnard after the crusading Columbia president. Though students at both Columbia and Barnard can take classes at each other's schools, Barnard remains a separate and proud institution.

Turn left on 120th Street, then right on Claremont Avenue, passing the **Union Theological Seminary** (turning out liberal Protestant ministers since 1836), to the unassuming main entrance on your left into:

9. **Riverside Church** (☎ 212/870-6712; www.theriver sidechurchny.org), just about the grandest Baptist church I've ever seen, built with John D. Rockefeller, Jr.'s money. Rockefeller was born a Baptist, but was a big believer in healing the rifts in Christianity, a philosophy called the interfaith movement, and the church to this day remains as much community center as house of worship, and its Interfaith Center offices host Christians, Jews, and Muslims.

Though the structure bears a passing resemblance to the French cathedral at Chartres and is festooned with Gothic frippery, this one's all modern, sporting a skeleton of steel girders that lets its tower soar to an incredible 392 feet. It's a big church, too: 265 feet long and 100 feet wide, with seating for 2,500, but the overall effect is light and airy, with some stellar stained glass windows, quality stone carvings, and one whopper of a sound system.

Riverside's famed carillon was first installed in 1925, its 53 bells making it the largest carillon in the nation. It kept that title (enlarged to 72 bells in 1931 with two more added in 1956) until 1960 when it slipped to second place (though it's still the heaviest set in the USA). It's played Sundays at 10:30am, 12:30pm, and 3pm (sometimes 2:30pm). The church is open daily 9am to 5pm.

Continue north on Claremont Avenue, to 122nd Street, where you turn left to cross Riverside Drive and pay your respects at:

10. **Grant's Tomb.** You'll never guess who's buried here! (Actually, Grant's wife is also interred here, so a lot of people get the answer to that famed nonriddle only half right.) The tomb of the only president buried in NYC is as bullet-headed as the man it honors, a giant round-peg-in-a-square-hole game with a colonnaded rotunda perched atop a square Classical temple, all topped off at 150 feet by a flattened cone for a roof. It's the largest tomb in America.

The 8,000 tons of marble are meant to resemble the Mausoleum at Halicarnassus. Inside, the associations continue with a design modeled after Napoléon's tomb in Paris, the white Carrara marble brightened with mosaics depicting the high points of Grant's military career, including the Surrender of Robert E. Lee at Appomattox (it's the one in which the two generals seem to be shaking hands amiably).

The hero of the Civil War and post-bellum President was still a very popular guy by the time he died in 1885, and 90,000 people contributed the $600,000 (and that's in 1890s dollars) to build this tomb. Ulysses and his wife, Julia Dent, are buried in the basement tomb. Above the entrance are Grant's famous words—all the more moving coming from a man of war—"Let us have peace." The tomb is open 9am to 5pm, with tours hourly until 4pm.

Cross back across Riverside Drive and down 122nd Street to Broadway. Across at the northeast corner you'll see the:

11. **Jewish Theological Seminary,** a neo-Georgian building houses this seminary, founded in the rather enlightened year of 1886 to train up passels of American rabbis. The library of 300,000 volumes comprises the largest collection of Judaica in the Western Hemisphere.

Turn right down Broadway. Between 121st and 120th streets, you'll pass the façade of the:

12. **Teacher's College.** In 1889, with all the future religious and secular leaders graduating from Columbia and neighboring seminaries, Nicholas Murray Butler decided New York could do with some quality educators to do the teaching. So he took the Kitchen Garden Club based at St-Mark's-in-the-Bowery (which was busy mucking about the public school system with a wonderfully ill-conceived program to train working-class girls on how to keep, if you'll pardon the expression, better homes and gardens), attached it to Columbia, and slowly evolved the operation into one of the nation's most progressive educational think-tanks, producing such luminaries as John Dewey.

Turn right on 120th Street to walk down the long side of the college all the way to Morningside Drive and:

13. **Morningside Park.** This is not so much a park by design as by force of nature: It's the schist cliff that separates lofty Morningside Heights from the lowlands of Harlem, part of the ridge of solid rock that rides along the spine of Manhattan island. Even New Yorkers didn't know how to make good real estate use of a cliff back in the middle of the 19th century, so master landscapists Frederick Law Olmsted and Calvert Vaux, of Central Park fame, were called in to beautify this strip of schist and trees.

The two loved the views from this natural balcony, and laid out their plans to make best use of it, but a guy named Jacob Mould butted in, started building bastions of masonry against the cliff, and threatened to ruin the whole setting. Luckily, after he kicked off, the Dream Team of park planners were brought back, and Vaux started doing what he could with what was left, planting small gardens, leaving craggy rock faces bare, fitting in stands of trees, and lacing it with a zigzag of pathways that lets you gently waft your way down from the Heights into Harlem.

Before plunging in, turn right down Morningside Drive to skirt the park for a bit, enjoying the sweeping views across Harlem, which you're about to plunge into. At 116th Street—where on the right at no. 60 you'll see the lovely 1912 McKim, Mead, and White–designed house of Columbia University's president—turn into the park itself and pick a path down the bluff to get the Harlem side of 116th Street.

The change in neighborhoods is dramatic, from elegant academia to dingy-but-vibrant urban. Take a few blocks to adjust as you continue east on 116th Street. Just before Lenox Avenue at no. 113, you'll find one of the best purveyors of soul food in New York.

Take a Break Amy Ruth's (☎ 212/280-8779; www.amyruth.com). Growing up, owner Carl Redding and his siblings spent summers on the farm in Alabama. While his brothers did farm chores, Carl stuck by the side of his grandmother, Amy Ruth, learning timeless soul food recipes from the world's leading expert: a black southern country grandma.

If you try nothing else, make sure someone orders their signature dish of fried chicken and waffles. Oh, and the bourbon-glazed Virginia ham. But then you also can't miss the smothered pork chops. And what about the fried catfish with sweet potato fries you can get on Fridays? Look, either bring a lot of friends or, better yet, make plans to come back a few times so you can work your way through the menu properly.

Amy Ruth's is open daily 7:30am to 11pm, staying open 24 hours Friday and Saturday nights, and the upstairs back room hosts a variety of events, including comedy performances, concerts, open mike nights, and more.

Across the street, at the southwest corner of the intersection of 116th Street and Lenox Avenue, sit the boxy yellow walls of the:

14. **Malcolm Shabazz Mosque No. 7,** a giant green onion dome perched atop a squat shape that harks back to its origins as the Lenox Casino. Elijah Muhammad turned it into the Temple of Islam in 1965, and Malcolm X was a resident preacher until his break with the movement.

Cross Lenox Avenue and walk down the south side of 116th Street half a block to the:

15. **Malcolm Shabazz Harlem Market,** a colorful outdoor bazaar of tiny shops and stalls hawking West African crafts and Harlem souvenirs.

Double back to Lenox Avenue and turn right (north) up it, past (at no. 130) the recently-finished (it opened in 2000) *The Renaissance,* a low-income co-op of 241 apartments, with parking, ringed on the ground level by 60,000 square feet of retail space, all part of the neighborhood's recent revival efforts. At 120th Street, where the **Mount Olivet Baptist Church** (built in 1907 as a Jewish Temple) rises on the corner, turn right to enter the core of the:

16. **Mount Morris Historic District,** a clutch of 19th-century brownstones between 119th and 123rd and one of the first New York neighborhoods to be declared a Historic District (in 1971). The area is slowly being

rehabilitated and renovated to its former glory. The street spills into the southwest corner of:

17. **Marcus Garvey Park.** This gnarly outcropping of Manhattan mica-schist was just too darn hard to level for development, plus it made a handy lookout point. Were you to scrape away Manhattan's skyscrapers and other buildings, the pinnacle of this park would be one of the highest points on the island, used as a lookout point by everyone from Indian tribes to the 19th-century fire department. In fact, their iron watchtower from 1865 still perches atop the highest point, 10,000-pound bell and all, the only such tower to remain in the city (great views from the top).

The park was renamed in 1973 to honor the famed local black activist Marcus Garvey.

Walk north along Mount Morris Park West and turn left at 122nd Street. Cross Lenox Avenue and continue west on 122nd Street onto:

18. **Doctor's Row,** a lovely stretch of row homes (though a few brownstones are still boarded up) from the late 1800s. The best are nos. 133–143, a lovely row of ornate brick homes built by Francis H. Kimball in 1885–87, the best Queen Anne–style homes surviving in all of Manhattan, a brick festival of gables, dormers, decoration, and stained glass.

At the far end of the block on the south side, at no. 152–154, is the:

19. **Hale House,** established in 1969 by Mother Clara Hale to provide aid for drug-addicted (and now also HIV-infected) infants and their mothers. In 1996, four years after Hale's death, sculptor Robert Berks memorialized Mother Hale in a sculpture surrounded by etched bronze plaques of children.

Turn right up Adam Clayton Powell Jr. Boulevard to head north. Turn right onto:

20. **125th Street,** the bustling, vibrant heart of the new Harlem renaissance, the epicenter of a development boom in the past few years. These 3 blocks are home to the Studio Museum, the Apollo Theater, the National Black

Theatre, the Harlem USA shopping complex, and a multiplex cinema owned by Magic Johnson. Is it any wonder Bill Clinton chose this hip-hop-happening spot for his postpresidential offices in New York? (Though it's my private opinion that he actually moved here for the soul food.)

Turn right and walk down about a quarter of the block to the:

21. **Studio Museum,** 144 W. 125th St. (☎ 212/864-4500; www.studiomuseum.org), a vast gallery space that since 1968 has been devoted to collecting, preserving, and promoting contemporary African-American art, both from Harlem, across the USA, and around the world. The bulk of its display space is taken up with rotating exhibits, though they also have a fine and growing collection. The gift shop is also quite excellent. The gallery hours are Sunday and Wednesday to Friday noon to 6pm, Saturday 10am to 6pm. Admission is $5, but free on the first Saturday of the month.

Continue toward the end of the block at Lenox Avenue. Across the street, along with a Chase bank, you'll see the 14-story office building of:

22. **55 W. 125th St.,** which became famous in 2001 when a new resident moved in and the top floor became the offices of former president Bill Clinton. After flirting with pricey Midtown digs, Clinton chose to put his money where his mouth was and move into the heart of Harlem, one of the Federal Empowerment Zones (a program that provides federal aid for economically depressed areas) that he himself created as president.

After all, Toni Morrison once called him "our first black president," pointing out the similarities between his upbringing (raised by a single mother, as a Baptist, on southern soul food and at the edge of poverty) and the experience of many in the black community. Not everyone buys that, but the fact is, the man does seem to be fitting in nicely enough.

Turn around to double back up 125th Street, cross Adam Clayton Powell Jr. Boulevard, cross to the north side of the street, and finish this tour with perhaps the best-known stop in Harlem. Folks, it's showtime at the:

23. **Apollo Theater,** 253 W. 125th St. (☎ 212/531-5305; www.apollotheater.com). The Apollo, like most old Harlem entertainment venues including the vanished Cotton Club, began life as a burlesque house open to whites only: Hurtig and Seamon's Music Hall, established in 1913. But in 1934, new owners Frank Schiffman and Leo Brecher threw open the doors to the local black community and a legend was born.

How do you even begin to pare down the list of musicians and entertainers who have graced the Apollo's stage? Bessie Smith, Count Basie, Billie Holiday, Louis Armstrong, Dizzy Gillespie, Duke Ellington, Charlie "Bird" Parker, Nat "King" Cole, Marvin Gaye, Bo Diddley, Gladys Knight (I assume with the Pips in tow), Aretha Franklin, Stevie Wonder, George Clinton, B. B. King, Prince . . . Look, just go to the R&B section of your local record store and read off the names, it might be quicker. When the Beatles invaded America in 1964, there was only one thing they wanted to see in New York City: the Apollo Theater. And I haven't even started in on the entertainers who didn't sing their way to fame (Redd Foxx, Whoopi Goldberg, Bill Cosby . . .).

The famous, and famously tough, Amateur Night at the Apollo (Wed at 7:30pm; tickets start at $16) has kick-started many careers, among them Ella Fitzgerald, James Brown, Lauryn Hill, Sarah Vaughn, and a little Motown group called the Jackson 5.

When a show is not on, you often can't enter the theater, but from the doorway you can see the stump of the Tree of Hope, which once grew outside the Lafayette Theater. Performers would kiss that tree (and, later, its replacement donated by Mr. Bojangles himself, the dancer Bill Robinson), and latter-day hopefuls always touch it for good luck before taking the stage.

Our walk officially ends here. Harlem continues all the way to 168th Street, but my feet are tired, and truth be told, the rest of Harlem doesn't lend itself well to walking. It tends to have points of touristic interest only every 10 blocks or so, with the interim spaces often depressingly depressed areas. However, I highly recommend you hop on the subway here at 125th Street and ride it one stop north to 135th Street to fit in a few more must-see Harlem stops.

Here you can visit a branch of the New York Public Library that has become the excellent **Schomburg Center for Research in Black Culture** at 515 Lenox Ave. The **Abyssinian Baptist Church** on 138th St. is famous for its Sunday morning gospel service and as the place where Adam Clayton Powell Jr. got his start, preaching in the pulpit here from 1938 before moving on to organize black boycotts of exclusionary businesses, hold a post on the city council, and eventually take a seat in the U.S. Congress.

Make sure you also stroll down 139th Street between Frederick Douglass Boulevard and Adam Clayton Powell Jr. Boulevard, a lovely stretch of row houses in dark brick Italianate style on the north side and in yellow brick colonial revival style on the south side. It's officially part of the St. Nicholas Historic District, but is much better known as **Striver's Row** after the upwardly-mobile blacks and others who once made these blocks their home, including Memphis-born father of the blues W. C. Handy (232 W. 139th St.) and—appropriately enough, given the gorgeous surroundings—Vertner Tandy, the first black architect registered in New York State (221 W. 139th St.).

As long as you're up here you can fit in some more soul food at Miss Maude's **Spoonbread Too** (☎ **212/690-3100**) at 547 Lenox Ave. between 137th and 138th streets. Southern fried chicken, Carolina-style barbecued ribs, golden fried shrimp, smothered pork chops, Louisiana catfish, collard greens, potato salad, candied yams, banana pudding, peach cobbler, sweet potato pie . . . Mmm . . . soul food.

Essentials

This chapter includes all the information you'll need to get your bearings in New York City.

ORIENTATION

Laid out on a grid system (except for the Village), Manhattan is the easiest of the boroughs to negotiate. Avenues run north (uptown) and south (downtown), and streets run east to west (crosstown). Broadway runs southeast to northwest diagonally across the grid.

Both avenues and streets are numbered consecutively: Streets are numbered from south to north (1st St. is downtown just above Houston St.), and avenues are numbered from east to west (with Fifth Ave. in the center), from First Avenue near the East River to Twelfth Avenue near the Hudson River. The only major exceptions are the three named avenues on the East Side: Madison (east of Fifth Ave.), Park (which would be Fourth Ave.), and Lexington (west of Third Ave.). Sixth Avenue is also now called the Avenue of the Americas, though die-hard New Yorkers refuse to call it that.

Fifth Avenue is the dividing line between the East Side and the West Side, so an address on West 43rd Street will be west of Fifth Avenue. All east-west street addresses are counted from Fifth Avenue, starting at no. 1 on either side of Fifth and increasing in number as they move away from Fifth Avenue. In other words, at the corner of Fifth Avenue and 35th Street, you'll find 1 E. 35th St. to the east and 1 W. 35th St to the west. Street addresses increase by about 50 per block starting at Fifth Avenue. For example, nos. 1 to 50 East are just about between Fifth and Madison avenues, while nos. 1 to 50 West are just about between Fifth and Sixth avenues. Therefore 28 W. 23rd St. is a short walk west of Fifth Avenue; 325 E. 35th St. would be a few blocks east of Fifth.

A few avenues acquire new names as they move uptown: Eighth Avenue becomes Central Park West above 59th Street, Ninth Avenue becomes Columbus Avenue above 69th Street, and Tenth Avenue becomes Amsterdam above 72nd Street. Beware: Avenue addresses are irregular. For example, 994 Second Ave. is at East 51st Street, but so is 320 Park Ave. Thus, it's important to know a building's cross street to find it easily.

The handy grid pattern wasn't imposed on the older downtown sections below 14th Street on the West Side or below Houston Street on the East Side. Downtown streets have names rather than numbers, and in the oldest sections, roads follow the old street plans of "Nieuw Amsterdam" and the various small villages and farms surrounding it that long ago joined together to become New York City.

VISITOR INFORMATION

BEFORE YOU GO

For information before you leave home, a great source is **NYC & Company,** the organization that fronts the New York Convention & Visitors Bureau (NYCVB), 810 Seventh Ave., New York, NY 10019. You can call ☎ **800/NYC-VISIT** or 212/397-8222 to order the **Official NYC Visitor Kit,** which contains the *Official NYC Guide* detailing hotels, restaurants, theaters, attractions, events, and more; a foldout map; a decent newsletter on the latest goings-on in the city; and brochures on attractions and services. It costs $5.95 to receive the packet (payable by credit card) in 7 to 10 days, $9.95 for rush delivery (3–4 business days) to U.S. addresses and international orders. (*Note:* We have received complaints that packages don't always strictly adhere to these time frames.)

You can also find a wealth of free information on the bureau's website, **www.nycvisit.com**. To speak with a travel counselor who can answer specific questions, call ☎ **212/484-1222,** which is staffed daily weekdays from 8:30am to 6pm EST, weekends from 9am to 5pm EST.

For British visitors, the **NYCVB Visitor Information Center** is at 33-34 Carnaby St., London W1F 7DW (☎ **0207/437-8300**). You can order the Official NYC Visitor Kit by sending an A5-size self-addressed envelope and 72p postage to the above address.

WHEN YOU ARRIVE

The **Times Square Visitors Center,** 1560 Broadway, between 46th and 47th streets (where Broadway meets Seventh Ave.), across from the TKTS booth on the east side of the street (☎ 212/768-1560; www.timessquarebid.org), is the city's top info stop. This pleasant and attractive center features a helpful info desk offering loads of citywide information. There's also a tour desk selling tickets for Gray Line bus tours and Circle Line boat tours; a Metropolitan Transportation Authority (MTA) desk staffed to sell MetroCard fare cards, provide public transit maps, and answer all of your questions on the transit system; a Broadway Ticket Center providing show information and selling full-price show tickets; ATMs and currency exchange machines; and computer terminals with free Internet access courtesy of Yahoo! It's open daily from 8am to 8pm.

The New York Convention and Visitors Bureau runs the **NYCVB Visitor Information Center** at 810 Seventh Ave., between 52nd and 53rd streets. In addition to loads of information on citywide attractions and a multilingual counselor on hand to answer questions, the center also has interactive terminals that provide free touch-screen access to visitor information via Citysearch and sells advance tickets to major attractions, which can save you from standing in long ticket lines once you arrive. There's also an ATM, a gift shop, and phones that connect you directly with American Express card member services. The center is open Monday through Friday from 8:30am to 6pm, Saturday and Sunday from 9am to 5pm. For over-the-phone assistance, call ☎ 212/484-1222.

For comprehensive listings of films, concerts, performances, sporting events, museum and gallery exhibits, street fairs, and special events, the following are your best bets:

- The *New York Times* (**www.nytimes.com** or www.ny today.com) features terrific arts and entertainment coverage, particularly in the two-part Friday "Weekend" section and the Sunday "Arts & Leisure" section. Both days boast full guides to the latest happenings in Broadway and Off-Broadway theater, classical music, dance, pop and jazz, film, and the art world. Friday is particularly good for cabaret, family fun, and general-interest recreational and sightseeing events.

- *Time Out New York* (**www.timeoutny.com**) is my favorite weekly magazine. Dedicated to weekly goings-on, it's attractive, well organized, and easy to use. *TONY* features excellent coverage in all categories, from live music, theater, and clubs (gay and straight) to museum shows, dance events, book and poetry readings, and kids' stuff. The regular "Check Out" section, unequaled in any other listings magazine, will fill you in on upcoming sample and close-out sales, crafts and antiques shows, and other shopping-related scoops. A new issue hits newsstands every Thursday.

- The free weekly *Village Voice* (**www.villagevoice.com**), the city's legendary alterna-paper, is available late Tuesday downtown and early Wednesday in the rest of the city. From classical music to clubs, the arts and entertainment coverage couldn't be more extensive, and just about every live music venue advertises its shows here.

GETTING AROUND

BY SUBWAY

Run by the **Metropolitan Transit Authority (MTA),** the much-maligned subway system is actually the fastest way to travel around New York, especially during rush hours. Some 3.5 million people a day seem to agree with me, as it's their primary mode of transportation. The subway is quick, inexpensive, relatively safe, and pretty efficient, as well as being a genuine New York experience.

The subway runs 24 hours a day, 7 days a week. The rush-hour crushes are roughly from 8 to 9:30am and from 5 to 6:30pm on weekdays; the rest of the time the trains are relatively uncrowded.

For transit information, call the Metropolitan Transit Authority's **MTA/New York City Transit's Travel Information Center** at ☎ **718/330-1234.** For online information that's always up-to-the-minute current, visit **www.mta.nyc.ny.us**.

Paying Your Way The subway fare is $1.50 (half price for seniors and those with disabilities), and children under 44 inches tall ride free (up to three per adult). *Note:* As of this writing, a fare increase was being discussed, so it's entirely possible that the fare will be higher by the time you visit.

While **tokens** still exist (although they'll soon be phased out altogether), most people pay fares with the **MetroCard,** a magnetically encoded card that debits the fare when swiped through the turnstile (or the fare box on any city bus). Once you're in the system, you can transfer freely to any subway line that you can reach without exiting your station. Metro Cards—not tokens—also allow you **free transfers** between the bus and subway within a 2-hour period.

MetroCards can be purchased from each station's staffed token booth, where you can only pay with cash; at the ATM-style vending machines now located in just about every subway station in the city, which accept cash, credit cards, and debit cards; from a MetroCard merchant, such as most Rite Aid drugstores or Hudson News at Penn Station and Grand Central Terminal; or at the MTA information desk at the Times Square Visitor Center, 1560 Broadway, between 46th and 47th streets.

MetroCards come in a few different configurations:

Pay-Per-Ride MetroCards, which can be used for up to four people by swiping up to four times (bring the whole family). You can put any amount from $3 (two rides) to $80 on your card. Every time you put $15 on your Pay-Per-Ride MetroCard, it's automatically credited 10%—that's one free ride for every $15. You can buy Pay-Per-Ride MetroCards in any denomination at any subway station; an increasing number of stations now have automated MetroCard vending machines, which allow you to buy MetroCards using your major credit card. MetroCards are also available from shops and newsstands around town in $15 and $30 values. You can refill your card at any time until the expiration date on the card, usually about a year from the date of purchase, at any subway station.

Unlimited-Ride MetroCards, which can't be used for more than one person at a time or more frequently than 18-minute intervals, are available in four values: the **daily Fun Pass,** which allows you a day's worth of unlimited subway and bus rides for $4; the **7-Day MetroCard,** for $17; and the **30-Day MetroCard,** for $63. Seven- and 30-day Unlimited-Ride MetroCards can be purchased at any subway station or a MetroCard merchant. Fun Passes, however, cannot be purchased at token booths—you can only buy them at a MetroCard vending machine; from a MetroCard merchant; at the MTA information desk at the Times Square Visitor Center; or from www.metrocard.citysearch.com. Unlimited-Ride MetroCards go into effect not at the time you buy them but the first time you use them—so if you buy a card on Monday and don't begin to use it until Wednesday, Wednesday is when the clock starts ticking on your MetroCard. A Fun Pass is good from the first time you use it until 3am the next day, while 7- and 30-day MetroCards run out at midnight on the last day. These MetroCards cannot be refilled; throw them out once they've been used up and buy a new one.

If you're not sure how much money you have left on your MetroCard, or what day it expires, use the station's MetroCard Reader, usually located near the station entrance or the token booth (on buses, the fare box will also provide you with this information).

To locate the nearest MetroCard merchant, or for any other MetroCard questions, call ☎ **800/METROCARD** or 212/METROCARD (212/638-7622) Monday through Friday between 7am and 11pm, Saturday and Sunday from 9am to 5pm. Or go online to **www.mta.nyc.ny.us/metrocard**, which can give you a full rundown of MetroCard merchants in the tristate area.

See the subway map on the back inside cover of this book to figure out your route.

BY BUS

Less expensive than taxis and more pleasant than subways (they provide a mobile sightseeing window on Manhattan), MTA buses are a good transportation option. Their very big drawback: They can get stuck in traffic, sometimes making it quicker to walk. They also stop every couple of blocks, rather than the 8 or 9 blocks that local subways traverse between stops. So for long distances, the subway is your best bet; but for short distances or traveling crosstown, try the bus.

Paying Your Way   Like the subway fare, **bus fare** is $1.50, half price for seniors and riders with disabilities, free for children under 44 inches (up to three per adult). The fare is payable with a **MetroCard,** a **token** (for now, anyway), or **exact change.** Bus drivers don't make change, and fare boxes don't accept dollar bills or pennies. You can't purchase MetroCards or tokens on the bus, so you'll have to have them before you board; for details on where to get them, see "Paying Your Way" under "By Subway," above.

If you pay with a MetroCard, you can transfer to another bus or to the subway for free within 2 hours. If you use a token, you must request a **free transfer** slip that allows you to change to an intersecting bus route only (legal transfer points are listed on the transfer paper) within 1 hour of issue. Transfer slips cannot be used to enter the subway.

Using the System   You can't flag a city bus down—you have to meet it at a bus stop. **Bus stops** are located every 2 or 3 blocks on the right-side corner of the street (facing the direction of traffic flow). They're marked by a curb painted yellow and a blue-and-white sign with a bus emblem and the route number or numbers. Guide-A-Ride boxes at most stops display a route map and a hysterically optimistic schedule.

Almost every major avenue has its own **bus route.** They run either north or south: downtown on Fifth, uptown on Madison, downtown on Lexington, uptown on Third, and so on. There are **crosstown buses** at strategic locations all around town: 8th Street (eastbound); 9th (westbound); 14th, 23rd, 34th, and 42nd (east- and westbound); 49th (eastbound); 50th (westbound); 57th (east- and westbound); 65th (eastbound across the West Side, through the park, and then north on Madison, continuing east on 68th to York Ave.); 67th (westbound on the East Side to Fifth Ave. and then south on Fifth, continuing west on 66th St. through the park and across the West Side to West End Ave.); and 79th, 86th, 96th, 116th, and 125th (east- and westbound).

Most routes operate 24 hours a day, but service is infrequent at night. During rush hour, main routes have "limited" buses, identifiable by the red card in the front window; they stop only at major cross streets.

To make sure the bus you're boarding goes where you're going, check the maps on the sign that's at every bus stop, get your hands on a route & Subway map, or just ask.

Signal for a stop by pressing the tape strip above and beside the windows and along the metal straps, about 2 blocks before you want to stop. Exit through the pneumatic back doors (not the front door) by pushing on the yellow tape strip; the doors open automatically. Most city buses are equipped with wheelchair lifts, making buses the preferable mode of public transportation for wheelchair-bound travelers. Buses also "kneel," lowering down to the curb to make boarding easier.

Index

FROMMER'S® MEMORABLE WALKS

Chicago	New York	San Francisco
London	Paris	Washington, D.C.

FROMMER'S® GREAT OUTDOOR GUIDES

Arizona & New Mexico	Northern California	Vermont & New Hampshire
New England	Southern New England	

SUZY GERSHMAN'S BORN TO SHOP GUIDES

Born to Shop: France	Born to Shop: Italy	Born to Shop: New York
Born to Shop: Hong Kong, Shanghai & Beijing	Born to Shop: London	Born to Shop: Paris

FROMMER'S® IRREVERENT GUIDES

Amsterdam	Los Angeles	San Francisco
Boston	Manhattan	Seattle & Portland
Chicago	New Orleans	Vancouver
Las Vegas	Paris	Walt Disney World®
London	Rome	Washington, D.C.

FROMMER'S® BEST-LOVED DRIVING TOURS

Britain	Germany	Northern Italy
California	Ireland	Scotland
Florida	Italy	Spain
France	New England	Tuscany & Umbria

HANGING OUT™ GUIDES

Hanging Out in England	Hanging Out in France	Hanging Out in Italy
Hanging Out in Europe	Hanging Out in Ireland	Hanging Out in Spain

THE UNOFFICIAL GUIDES®

Bed & Breakfasts and Country Inns in:
- California
- Great Lakes States
- Mid-Atlantic
- New England
- Northwest
- Rockies
- Southeast
- Southwest

Best RV & Tent Campgrounds in:
- California & the West
- Florida & the Southeast
- Great Lakes States
- Mid-Atlantic
- Northeast
- Northwest & Central Plains
- Southwest & South Central Plains
- U.S.A.

Beyond Disney
Branson, Missouri
California with Kids
Chicago
Cruises
Disneyland®
Florida with Kids
Golf Vacations in the Eastern U.S.
Great Smoky & Blue Ridge Region
Inside Disney
Hawaii
Las Vegas
London

Mid-Atlantic with Kids
Mini Las Vegas
Mini-Mickey
New England and New York with Kids
New Orleans
New York City
Paris
San Francisco
Skiing in the West
Southeast with Kids
Walt Disney World®
Walt Disney World® for Grown-ups
Walt Disney World® with Kids
Washington, D.C.
World's Best Diving Vacations

SPECIAL-INTEREST TITLES

Frommer's Adventure Guide to Australia & New Zealand
Frommer's Adventure Guide to Central America
Frommer's Adventure Guide to India & Pakistan
Frommer's Adventure Guide to South America
Frommer's Adventure Guide to Southeast Asia
Frommer's Adventure Guide to Southern Africa
Frommer's Britain's Best Bed & Breakfasts and Country Inns
Frommer's Caribbean Hideaways
Frommer's Exploring America by RV
Frommer's Fly Safe, Fly Smart
Frommer's France's Best Bed & Breakfasts and Country Inns
Frommer's Gay & Lesbian Europe

Frommer's Italy's Best Bed & Breakfasts and Country Inns
Frommer's New York City with Kids
Frommer's Ottawa with Kids
Frommer's Road Atlas Britain
Frommer's Road Atlas Europe
Frommer's Road Atlas France
Frommer's Toronto with Kids
Frommer's Vancouver with Kids
Frommer's Washington, D.C., with Kids
Israel Past & Present
The New York Times' Guide to Unforgettable Weekends
Places Rated Almanac
Retirement Places Rated

You Need A Vacation.

700 Airlines, 50,000 Hotels, 50 Rental Car
Companies, And A Million Ways To Save Money.

Travelocity.com
A S a b r e C o m p a n y
Go Virtually Anywhere.